Teresa M.

Sunset
International Vegetarian
Cook Book

By the Editors of Sunset Books and Sunset Magazine

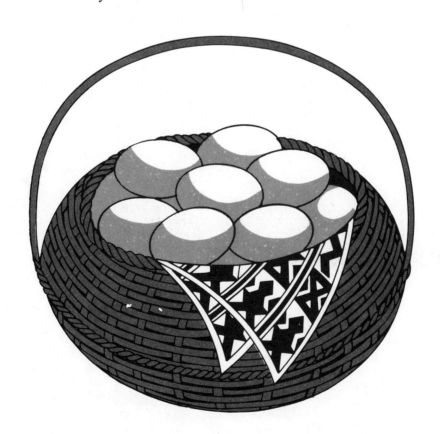

Lane Publishing Co. ● Menlo Park, California

*Christmas 2016
from Mom*

Supervising Editor
Maureen Williams Zimmerman

Research & Text
Sharon Cadwallader
Cynthia Scheer
Susan Warton
Elizabeth Friedman
Claire Coleman

Design
Joe di Chiarro

Illustrations
H. Tom Kamifuji

Photography
Nikolay Zurek

Photo Editor
Lynne B. Morrall

Our international banquet . . .

of great-tasting vegetarian dishes comes from the following places around the globe: Argentina • Armenia • Barbados • Belgium • Bulgaria • Canada • the Caribbean • China • Denmark • Ecuador • Egypt • Ethiopia • Finland • France • Germany • Greece • Guatemala • Holland • Hungary • India • Ireland • Israel • Italy • Jamaica • Japan • Lebanon • Luxembourg • Mexico • Morocco • Nicaragua • Norway • the Orient • Poland • Polynesia • Portugal • Russia • Scandinavia • Scotland • Sicily • Spain • Sweden • Switzerland • Thailand • Tunisia • Turkey • U.S.A. • Venezuela • Vietnam • Wales • the West Indies • Yugoslavia

Our special thanks . . .

go to Dr. Ann Burroughs, University of California at Berkeley, for answering our questions about nutrition. And for their generosity in sharing props for the photographs, we extend special thanks to Taylor & Ng, Williams–Sonoma Kitchenware, and Woodside Deli.

Cover: In a summery symphony of garden-fresh flavor, eggplant, peppers, zucchini, spinach, and tomatoes mingle with herbs in France's classic *ratatouille* (recipe on page 39). For flourish, we added garnishes of lemon zest and fresh basil. Photograph by Nikolay Zurek. Cover design by Lynne B. Morrall.

Editor, Sunset Books: David E. Clark

First printing April 1983

Contents

Special Features

Vegetarian Ways Around the World

Traditional cuisines offer interest, variety

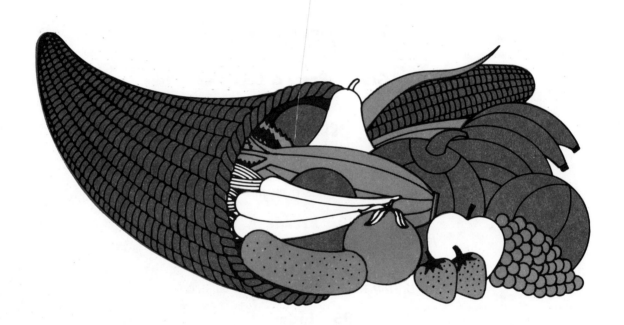

Contemporaries of George Bernard Shaw probably smiled and shook their heads at his contrary view of fine English roast mutton. But his delight in fresh greens and whole grains— and his rejection of eating meat—would not lift an eyebrow today.

A meatless diet, at one time considered an eccentricity, is becoming more and more a matter of course. Some people give up meat completely for reasons ranging from personal philosophy to interest in nutrition to concern about high grocery bills. Many others simply veer in a vegetarian direction—maybe to cut down on animal fat and cholesterol, or maybe just from the influence of a vegetarian spouse, friend, son, or daughter.

Whichever route has brought you to meatless cooking, be prepared for exciting adventures with new, fresh flavors. You'll want a large repertoire of good recipes to make the most of the array of natural foods that go into this style of cooking. And that's what you'll find here, in abundance, from such intriguing places as Bulgaria, Jamaica, Thailand, and Egypt—to name but a few sources for our recipes.

Our quest for new ideas to expand upon the popular theme of Sunset's earlier vegetarian cook book, *Menus & Recipes for Vegetarian Cooking*, led us, inevitably, to other countries. It seemed a natural progression to pair vegetarian cooking with international recipes.

Though our recipes were inspired by ethnic ingredients and methods of preparation, we've made some changes in the interest of contemporary knowledge of nutrition and availability of ingredients, and sometimes for an extra fillip for American taste buds.

Food Wisdom from Other Cultures

Today, many nutritionists point out that in countries that are less developed but where food is plentiful, people generally partake of more nourishing fare than we do in the United States, in spite of the availability of nutritious food in this country. That same nutritional wisdom turns up in much of the country cooking of Europe—generally a high-carbohydrate offering of fresh foods, locally raised. This more healthful food meets needs without excess calories or protein, and without the potentially harmful load of salt, refined sugar, and additives that go into refined and processed foods.

Variations on common themes worldwide

Cooking styles vary wonderfully from one region of the globe to another. Still, we quickly discovered common themes, all in line with nutritional wisdom upheld by modern research.

Everywhere, it seems, people respect food, make the most of everything available, and work imaginative variety into the serving of staples. All the range of soy products used in Far Eastern kitchens is one example. Notice, too, how the Japanese honor seasonal produce in Vegetable Tempura (page 26), or how the Greeks waste nothing of their indigenous grape vines, a delicious thrift typified in Stuffed Grape Leaves (page 14).

Whether it's a Chinese stir-fried mixture or a Bedouin eggplant stew, many traditional cuisines mix a healthy variety of vegetables (along with nuts, seeds, or fruits) in one main dish. In the Caribbean, or in the Balkans, this mostly vegetarian medley often tops a hefty mound of grain or is eaten with fresh-baked whole grain bread.

The high-protein combination of grains with legumes, explained further along, appears in sup-

Choosing Nutritiously

Vitamins & Minerals	Main Sources	Vitamins & Minerals	Main Sources
A	Apricots, broccoli, butternut squash, cantaloupe, carrots, dark leafy greens, Hubbard squash, papaya, red bell pepper, sweet potato	Niacin	Bulgur wheat, collards, cottage cheese, fresh and dried peas, kidney beans, lentils, navy beans, pinto beans, soybeans, tofu
D	Egg yolk, fortified milk	B-6	Avocado, bananas, black-eyed peas, buckwheat flour, garbanzos, kale, lentils, pinto beans, soybeans
E	Almonds, beet greens, filberts, spinach, sweet potato, unsaturated oils (especially safflower, sunflower, and walnut), walnuts, wheat germ	Folic Acid	Brewer's yeast, garbanzos, kidney beans, limas, oranges, rye flour, soybeans, spinach, sweet potato, whole wheat flour
C	Broccoli, Brussels sprouts, cantaloupe, cauliflower, citrus juice, kale, oranges, papaya, parsley, red and green bell pepper, strawberries	B-12	Cheese (such as blue, Camembert, Cheddar, Edam, mozzarella), cottage cheese, eggs, milk, yogurt
Thiamin (B-1)	Barley, brewer's yeast, green peas, navy beans, pinto beans, soybeans, spinach, wheat berries, wheat germ, whole wheat flour	Calcium	Bok choy, broccoli, collards, corn tortillas, dairy products, kale, mustard greens, okra, soybeans
Riboflavin (B-2)	Asparagus, broccoli, butternut squash, Camembert cheese, collards, cottage cheese, milk, mushrooms, okra, yogurt	Iron	Black beans, dried peas, garbanzos, lentils, limas, navy beans, pinto beans, prune juice, soybeans, spinach

pers served almost everywhere. ("Legumes" and "pulses" are more scientific terms for dried beans, lentils, split peas, and peanuts; the more familiar terms "grains" and "cereals" refer to rice and wheat, and to products of these and other grains— products such as pasta, porridge, or bread.) Lebanon's Lentil & Bulgur Pilaf (page 50) has a parallel in Guatemala's Zesty Black Bean Tacos (page 76).

Dairy products and eggs also fill important roles worldwide. In one area, dairy food comes mainly in the form of cheese; in another, it's likely to be yogurt, artfully worked into cooling drinks, soups, sauces, salads, and such condiments as India's Cucumber Raita (page 54). An egg shines as a work of art in Japan's Shiitake Egg Drop Soup (page 29), and several eggs become a hearty sheepherders' meal in Basque Scrambled Eggs (page 59).

When they're not used in cooking, fruits and nuts around the world easily fill the niche nature must have intended for them—to be enjoyed as easy snacks, packaged plump with nourishment, and as lightly sweet and simple desserts.

The ideal—quality, variety, moderation

Many dietary customs of other cultures include those food groups just discussed—as, indeed, must any wholesome diet, whether eaten in Bangkok, Bucharest, or Birmingham.

Ingredients themselves have to be of good quality, obviously, if we're to gain the most from them. We now understand that much of this nutritional quality gets lost in the refinement process (as, for example, the valuable husk and germ disappear from brown rice when it's processed into white rice).

Enjoying a wide variety of foods is the best way to avoid any deficiency, without having to think much about it—provided the quality is good. Each apple, kidney bean, or broccoli spear, along with other whole foods, contains an individual kaleidoscope of vitamins, minerals, starch, and the amino acids that make up protein (more about these on the facing page). From each, you get a smattering of this to a heaping dose of that.

Variety, built into most traditional cuisines, presents no problem to anyone who is open to trying new flavors. And it should come naturally into your cooking, once you taste a few dishes from this book.

Moderation, the rule of thumb for avoiding excess weight, is a by-product of variety. Too much of one food (in lieu of wide variety), even if it is wholesome, can lead to trouble. Too many green apples can promise a stomachache, as surely as too many bowls of bran may so speed up digestion that vitamins and minerals can't be absorbed.

What Makes a Diet Balanced?

"Eat sensibly," we all heard as we grew up, knowing it had to do with more milk, oranges, and spinach and fewer cooky binges. If we're sticking to the principles of quality, variety, and moderation then we're already eating sensibly.

A balanced diet simply covers all nutritional needs adequately without overdoing things. It supplies carbohydrate sufficient for energy needs; essential vitamins and minerals, continually replenished as needed, for all kinds of metabolic work; and protein for the body's maintenance and repair (as well as growth in the early years).

Carbohydrate, fiber & fat

In other cultures, high-carbohydrate—starchy— foods tend to make up the bulk of the diet, in the form of staples: rice in the Far East; potatoes, wheat, and rye in Europe; corn in the Americas.

In a vegetarian regimen, many of these starchy staples do double duty as protein suppliers; Jamaica's Black Bean & Rice Soup (page 37), for example, boosts you with a supply of energy as it simultaneously provides as much protein as a moderate portion of meat. Into the bargain, too, many starchy foods contribute vitamins and minerals, along with valuable fiber (which, though it doesn't nourish, aids digestion).

Since we measure energy in calories, it's easy to leap to the conclusion that "starchy" means the same as "fattening." In truth, most of nature's high-carbohydrate foods come with only a moderate number of calories per serving, though we're accustomed to loading some of them (like potatoes) with rich toppings, adding considerably to the caloric content.

Fats certainly can be fattening, taken in excess. But without a small amount of fat, our bodies couldn't absorb the fat-soluble vitamins A, D, K, and E, nor would we get linoleic acid, another essential nutrient. The richest sources of linoleic acid, and lowest in cholesterol, are plant-derived fats, like the salad oils described on page 25.

In butter, cheese, and eggs, the fat is higher in cholesterol; but again, taken moderately (especially in a meatless diet that, in itself, cuts out a lot of cholesterol) these aren't likely to harm most people. If in doubt about cholesterol or any other point about nutrition, let your doctor guide you.

Vitamins & minerals

Foods rich in essential vitamins and minerals are listed on page 5. Among the richest are fruits and vegetables, but a few nutrients come mostly from grains, legumes, and dairy products.

Vegans—strict vegetarians who eat neither eggs nor dairy products—would be wise to check with their doctor to assure adequate amounts of riboflavin and B-12, both of which may be scarce for them otherwise. (Since a vegan diet can lead to other deficiencies, especially of protein, it's not recommended for children and pregnant or lactating women; and without a great deal of care, it's chancy for anyone.)

Protein for vegetarians

The issue of protein in vegetarianism has stirred up a lot of questions, and even hot controversy. Do you get enough protein without meat? What's the difference between plant and animal protein?

Like calorie allowances, protein need varies from one individual to another, shifting slightly from week to week and markedly through a lifetime; there's just no exact answer to how much everyone needs. As for protein quality in a vegetarian diet, when well planned, it may be superior to what we get from meat. Certainly it's less expensive; it may even lead to better health.

Protein requirements seem continually to ferment with revisions based on new research conclusions, but the most recent federal government "recommended dietary allowances" report shows that we probably need much less than we've believed heretofore. For example, a man of average size may consume 100 to 150 grams of protein through a normal breakfast, lunch, and

Protein Partnerships

For complete protein, combine a food from Column 2, 3, 4 with a different food from any other column. Foods in Column 1 provide complete protein by themselves.

1 No Limiting Amino Acid	2 Low in Lysine	3 Low in Sulfur-carrying Amino Acids	4 Low in Tryptophan

Dairy products
  Cheese (except cream
    cheese)
  Cottage cheese
  Milk (all types, including
    powdered)
  Yogurt
 	
Eggs
  Whole, and
  egg whites
 	
Legumes
  Soybeans
  Soybean curd (tofu)
  Soy flour
  Soy milk
  Tempeh
 	
Grains
  Wheat germ
 	
Nuts
  Walnuts, black
	Legumes
	  Peanuts
	
	Grains
	  Barley
	  Buckwheat
	  Bulgur
	  Cornmeal
	  Millet
	  Oats
	  Rice
	  Rye
	  Wheat
	
	Nuts & Seeds
	  Almonds
	  Brazil nuts
	  *Cashews
	  Coconut
	  Filberts
	  Pecans
	  Pumpkin seeds
	  Sunflower seeds
	  Walnuts, English
	
	Vegetables
	  Asparagus
	  Beet greens
	  Corn
	  Kale
	  Mushrooms
	  *Potatoes
	  Sweet potatoes
	  Yams
		Legumes
		  Beans, dried (black, pinto,
		    red, white)
		  Black-eyed peas, dried
		  Garbanzos
		  Lentils
		  Limas
		  Mung beans
		  *Peanuts
		
		Nuts
		  Filberts
		
		Vegetables
		  Asparagus
		  Beans, green
		  Beet greens
		  Broccoli
		  Brussels sprouts
		  Mushrooms
		  Parsley
		  Peas, green
		  Potatoes
		  Soybeans
		  Swiss chard
			Legumes
			  *Beans, dried (black, pinto,
			    red, white)
			  Garbanzos
			  Limas
			  Mung beans
			  *Peanuts
			
			Grains
			  Cornmeal
			
			Nuts
			  Almonds
			  Brazil nuts
			  *Walnuts, English
			
			Vegetables
			  Corn
			  Beet greens
			  Mushrooms
			  Peas, green
			  *Swiss chard

*Indicates foods containing more than 90 percent of ideal amount.

dinner, though his body really needs only about 55 grams of protein.

Making up a good proportion of what we are, from the hair on our heads to the toenails on our feet, protein works to keep us in good physical repair (and to aid growth, too, in children). Once this job is done, any excess becomes carbohydrate; then, if not burned as energy, it converts to fat, just as if it were an extra slice of chocolate cake. It is believed by most nutritionists that if we ate a little less protein, filling the deficit with more carbohydrate from grains, legumes, fruits, and vegetables, we'd be better off.

Essential amino acids. It's a common misconception to think we get "protein in the diet." What we really get are amino acids, which link up with more amino acids—inside our bodies, not on our plates—to create the protein that then becomes hair, fingernails, new skin, and other tissue.

Proteins are made up of chains of amino acids, most of them created by our bodies. Called "essential" are the amino acids that we must obtain from food. They must all be present at once to make protein.

All animal products, from eggs to herring, supply the full range of essential amino acids. But plant products come with a low amount of one or two (the exception is soybeans, which include them all in quantity). The low amino acids are called "limiting," since they do limit the usability of the final protein.

Complementary protein. By combining a food that's low in one or two essential amino acids with another food that's high in the same acids, you create a combination of high-quality protein, equivalent to that of meat. This is what happens in the grain-legume combinations mentioned earlier. Though grains tend to be low in lysine (one essential amino acid), legumes are high in it; simultaneously, the grains compensate for the limiting amino acid—tryptophan—in the legumes.

"Complementary protein" refers to this amino-acid pairing. Our Protein Partnerships chart (page 7) will guide you in creating complete-protein meals; we also make suggestions in recipes throughout the book. On the chart, we did not list all the amino acids, only the ones where a deficiency would make a difference.

A simple rule is to include milk, cheese, or eggs in your diet. Any of these compensate for the limitations of vegetable protein.

Calculating protein. Relax . . . there's no need to count every gram. Certainly vegetarians should know about protein complementarity, but take it all with a grain of salt (preferably sea salt). Babies, children, pregnant and lactating women, and people in a special health situation, like convalescence from a serious illness, do have special needs for amino acids. Extra care, under a doctor's guidance, should be taken in these cases.

For most adults, though, there's far less need to fuss with fancy calculations. Let your body guide you; if you look and feel hale and hearty, all's well—whether every gram of protein in your brown rice is "usable" or not. The idea of protein complementing quickly becomes basic to meal planning, without need for careful tallying.

Trying the Vegetarian Approach

If meatless meals are new to you, start by cutting back just on the quantity of meat you serve; then try one or two vegetarian dinners per week for a while. Some people give up red meat (highest in cholesterol and fat) while continuing to serve fish and poultry.

For people who are cutting back on—but not eliminating—meat from their diets, and for all the nonvegetarian family members and friends who share meals with vegetarians, we have provided, on the facing page, some suggestions for adding meat, fish, and poultry to the recipes in this book.

Is blandness unavoidable?

Certainly not, if you cook with enthusiasm and use exciting recipes—and we think every recipe in this book is exciting. Since a vegetarian meal is made up mostly of foods with relatively quiet natural flavors, vegetarian cooking calls for a bit of extra flair with seasonings or appealing combinations.

Each recipe in this book has been tested over and over again to bring out the most flavor without masking the natural delicacy of any ingredients. But we can't take all the credit. Our recipes are based on culinary traditions refined over centuries of pleasing people at the table, traditions that have already put most of the wonderful flavor into what you're about to enjoy. There seems to be a near-universal art in balancing the mild flavor of staples like potatoes or wheat with sprightly seasonings and other ingredients contrasting in color and texture. Caraway seeds, for example, brighten Tunisia's Potato Salad (page 24).

Certain regions are famous for their bold sauces or condiments. Mexico's Avocado Soup (page 36) brings festivity to the table with what you sprinkle on top, from the sliced green onions to the sour cream. Or if you favor a nip of heat, don't miss the Mandarin Pancakes with Spicy Tofu Filling (page 70) or North Africa's Vegetable-Bean Stew with

Couscous (page 42), which comes with a vibrant Hot Pepper Sauce.

Tips to save time & food value

Nothing ensures the nutritional value of produce like raising your own. But when back-yard goodness isn't possible, let freshness be your shopping guide; choose from what's in season and looks best.

Delicate salad or cooking greens should be rinsed, dried wrapped in paper towels, and sealed in plastic bags for storage in the refrigerator—but for only a day or two. Most other vegetables stay fresher if they're left unwashed and uncut until the last minute; store them, too, in plastic bags in the refrigerator.

Onions, garlic, and potatoes keep for a long time in a well-ventilated, dry area away from direct sunlight. Discard any potatoes that look greenish.

Grains, beans, nuts, and seeds became staple foods around the world partly because they stay fresh for long periods without refrigeration. Just keep them in sealed containers, away from direct sunlight. To save time, prepare grains or legumes in quantity, placing what you can't immediately use in recipe-size portions in airtight plastic containers. Store these for up to a week in the refrigerator, or for several months in the freezer.

When You Want to Add Meat

Many of the recipes in this book can be adapted for those who are gradually phasing out but are still eating meat, fish, and poultry—or who have no intention of giving these foods up at all. Actually, in their countries of origin, many of these recipes include meat when it's available, and omit it when it's not.

Allow about 4 ounces of meat per person. Sometimes, though, just a few slivers of fish or lamb give the flavor missed by meat eaters.

Appetizers. You can provide nibbles for both those who do and those who don't eat meat; simply add some cooked ham, cut into matchstick pieces, to part of the filling for Egg Rolls (page 15) before filling and frying them, or layer thinly sliced smoked salmon on each of the Chived Egg and Almond Canapés (page 14) from Norway.

Salads and vegetables. Add medium-size shrimp, shelled and deveined, to Vegetable Tempura (page 26). Coat and cook as directed for the vegetables.

Soups. Set aside a portion of soup for vegetarian diners; then add slivers of cooked ham to Thursday Pea Soup (page 36), slices of browned Italian sausage to Winter Minestrone (page 37), or slivers of cooked ham or boneless pork to Black Bean & Rice Soup (page 37).

Grains, pasta, and legumes. Offer hot cooked, boneless lamb or chicken strips alongside Vegetable-Bean Stew with Couscous (page 42).

Colorful Fried Rice (page 47) can be embellished easily with small cooked shrimp or with cooked ham cut into matchstick pieces; cook meat briefly with part of finished rice. To part of prepared filling for Kasha-stuffed Cabbage Rolls (page 42), add browned ground pork before enclosing filling in leaves. Or brown lean ground beef and add it to all or part of tomato sauce for Spinach Lasagne (page 53).

Eggs and cheese. Make Egg Foo Yung (page 60) with a few medium-size shrimp (shelled, deveined, and chopped), cook the shrimp separately, then mix with all or part of the vegetables before adding eggs. Crumble a few strips of cooked and drained bacon into half the prepared tart shell for Bernese Onion Tart (page 61) before adding the onion and egg mixture. Sprinkle some cooked chopped ham or cooked crumbled bacon atop Basque Scrambled Eggs (page 59).

Pancakes, crêpes, and tortillas. Zucchini Pancakes (page 72) can be complemented by grilled or broiled Italian sausages. Add lean, boneless pork, cut into matchstick pieces and cooked, to part of the filling for Mandarin Pancakes with Spicy Tofu Filling (page 70). Brown some lean ground beef and stir it into all or part of the Fresh Tomato Sauce for Spinach Ricotta Crêpes (page 73) or into a portion of the cooked beans for Zesty Black Bean Tacos (page 76) or Vegetable-Bean Tostadas (page 78); let diners choose from beans with or without meat when they assemble their entrées.

An International Menu Sampler

For everything from simple get-togethers with friends, to grand celebrations, parties, and picnics, here are vegetarian menu ideas to fire your imagination and whet your appetite.

Most bring together regional specialties from the same part of the world. And taken altogether, they are, deliciously, a gourmet tour of the globe—from Scandinavia, through Europe to the Middle East, on to Asia, across to the Americas.

Each menu is generous with protein, too, from a variety of superb-quality foods—eggs, dairy products, tofu, and complementary combinations of other foods. Strict vegetarians who don't eat eggs or dairy products will enjoy the elegant Vegan Dinner or the Sampler from the Far East.

Bear in mind, though, that protein isn't the only element in a menu that requires balancing. Consider color, flavor, and texture, as well. You wouldn't want to serve a meal where everything was soft, nor would you please everyone with a dinner of all spicy foods. Let our menus serve as a starting point, especially if vegetarian dining is new to you. In a short time, planning meatless meals will come easily.

Curry Feast

From India's Hindus, whose long vegetarian history dishes up some of the world's most glorious meatless delicacies, comes this colorful feast for six. It's as sparkling to the eye as to the palate. Cool, yogurty *raita* and chewy *chapaties* balance the spicy fire of the curry and chutney.

Potato & Egg Curry (page 44)
Cucumber Raita (page 54)
Mango Chutney (page 55)
Chapaties (page 81)
Cold Beer
Sliced Fresh Fruit (papaya, strawberries, kiwi) with Ginger Yogurt (page 90)
Indian Spiced Tea (page 93)

Lazy Morning Breakfast

Save this hearty and delicious menu for a slow morning when you can linger as long as you please over an extra scone or cup of coffee, lazy conversation or the Sunday paper. Serves four.

Fresh Melon Wedges
Cheese & Vegetable Omelet (page 57)
Toasted Whole Wheat Seed Bread (page 86)
Raisin Scones (page 83)
Butter and Jam or Marmalade
Coffee or Tea

Midnight Supper

To top off an evening of theater, Russia's elegant miniature pancakes—glistening with sour cream, slivered onions, chopped hard-cooked eggs, and dill weed—elegantly revive four sleepy people. Or save this menu to ring in the New Year. Champagne and Norway's bright carrot soup round out a beautiful light supper, followed by a rich, nutty dessert.

Blini (page 69)
Champagne
Carrot & Rice Soup (page 32)
Fresh Fruit
Filbert Chocolate Bars (page 92)

Latin American Dinner

Flavors from south of the border bring festivity to a dinner for six that's sure to inspire happy memories. Both the colorful soup and the zesty tacos require some last-minute attention, but the tacos can be prepared ahead, up to the final reheating. Citrus-sweetened bananas offer a gentle ending to the spicy repast.

Avocado Soup with Condiments (page 36)
Zesty Black Bean Tacos (page 76)
Bananas Managua (page 89)
Sangria (page 17)
Latin Coffee (page 93)

Vegan Dinner

Those who don't eat eggs or dairy products must take special care to pair foods that create complementary vegetable protein. If that sounds a little too scientific, just try this succulent example of spiced lentils and satisfying couscous. The menu for six is packed plump with complementary protein—but what you'll notice are the scintillating flavors.

Lentil Salad (page 48)
Vegetable Bean Stew with Couscous (page 42)
Whole Wheat Baguettes (page 83)
Fresh Pear Ice (page 94)

Harvest Celebration Brunch

Celebrate summer's zucchini abundance with this colorful brunch for four robust appetites. The crisp, green-flecked pancakes look and taste delicious topped with applesauce and sour cream. Golden muffins alongside complete a beautiful, fragrant, and good-tasting picture. And for anyone with room to spare, there's fresh pie made with one of summer's favorite fruits.

Zucchini Pancakes (page 72)
Sour Cream and Applesauce
Country Corn Muffins (page 81)
Peach & Sour Cream Pie (page 91)

Pasta Party

To entertain with ease, choose either Spinach Lasagne or Rolled Lasagne with Pesto (the spinach version can be made up to a day ahead). Six happy diners are sure to say "Bravo!"

Spinach Lasagne (page 53) or Rolled Lasagne
with Pesto (page 51)
Garlic Cheese Bread (page 85) or Italian Bread
Tossed Green Salad
Almond Crescents (page 92) and Fresh Fruit

Scandinavian Fireside Supper

In this cozy choice for wintertime—perhaps for the holiday season—hearty Scandinavian hors d'oeuvres cluster around warming soup for an informal fireside supper. Pass around the entrée and dessert soups in mugs, the hors d'oeuvres to eat with your fingers. Serves six.

Chived Egg & Almond Canapés (page 14)
Thursday Pea Soup (page 36)
Holiday Cheese Ball (page 13)
Scandinavian Crisp Rye Crackers
Mulled Wine (page 17)
Fresh Berry Soup (page 89)

Picnic from Eastern Europe

Slavic splendor from the kitchens of Bulgaria, Yugoslavia, and Hungary goes on a picnic. Rounding out the basket bounty for you and five other picnickers is Swedish rye bread (not exactly Slavic, but close—and, in any case, delicious).

Cucumber Walnut Soup (double recipe, page 31)
Dalmatian Rice & Caper Salad (page 41)
Eggplant & Pepper Salad (page 23)
Rye Bread (page 85, or purchased)
Cheese Pastries (page 92)

Middle Eastern Dinner

To add an authentic touch to this nomadic banquet, serve it on a blanket or rug (or a low table) with pillow seating. Take a Bedouin approach to the spread of food for six people by having everyone scoop up morsels from communal platters, using triangles of pocket bread.

Garbanzo Bean Dip (page 13)
Pocket Bread or Chapaties (page 81)
Bulgur & Mint Salad (page 41)
Mediterranean Lentil-Eggplant Stew (page 39)
Poached Apples with Almonds & Yogurt (page 89)
Turkish Coffee (page 93)

Sampler from the Far East

A soupçon of Japan, a dash of China, and a spicy sprinkling of Thailand co-mingle in this light but satisfying supper for four. (If you're a vegan, you can substitute Japan's Daikon Radish & Carrot Salad, on page 26, for the soup.)

Shiitake Egg Drop Soup (page 29)
Greens & Tofu in Peanut Sauce (page 48)
Hot Tea
Fresh Mandarin Oranges
Almond Cookies

Appetizers

A world of nourishing nibbles

To acquaint people with new foods, there's no more appealing "bait"—and none more assured of success—than a tempting array of appetizers. Because they're only bite-size, appetizers never seem so overwhelming as an entire exotic meal might. Offered informally from a tray or sideboard, they have the added advantage of leaving guests free to browse and select at a relaxed pace.

So whether it's the vegetarian or the international aspect that's new, we recommend starting off with a party. When the bite-size banquet is accompanied by one of the festive drinks listed on page 17, newfound flavors are all the more likely to become instant favorites.

Serve hors d' oeuvres before dinner, in the traditional manner—or add them to your menu in greater numbers and let them become a relaxed, roam-around meal in themselves. Entertain with a specific ethnic theme, if you prefer (a few suggestions follow), or simply mix cultures according to the ingredients you prefer.

For an easy Latin fiesta, offer Mexico's chile-sharp Nachos with sweet, colorful Onion Tarts from Spain. Let guests cool down the spicy heat of the Nachos with iced Sangria.

For a sampling from India, pair Potato-filled Pastries with Chutney Cheese Spread. Add a duo from the Orient—Egg Rolls from China and some of Japan's flavorful Miso Grilled Mushrooms. Or tour the Middle East with Lebanon's Garbanzo Bean Dip, which takes deliciously to pocket bread triangles or wheat crackers, as well as to crisp, raw vegetables.

From northern Europe comes hearty appetizer fare to banish the chill of winter. Around a fire, set out Egg & Almond Canapés from Norway; alongside, add Sweden's Holiday Cheese Ball. To go with either or both, offer Crisp-fried Onions from Denmark and steaming mugs of Mulled Wine from England.

These are only hints of the intriguing and delectable party foods coming up—foods that aren't likely to remain unfamiliar for long.

Garbanzo Bean Dip

Lebanon

A favorite partner for pocket bread throughout the Arab countries, this seasoned paste of garbanzo beans is known there as *hummus*. Spread it on triangles of either Chapaties (page 81) or pocket bread—or on wheat crackers or raw vegetables.

> 2 cups cooked garbanzo beans (page 49) or 1 can (15½ oz.) garbanzo beans (reserve liquid)
> 3 tablespoons sesame tahini (see page 41)
> 2 or 3 cloves garlic, minced or pressed
> 3 tablespoons lemon juice
> ⅛ teaspoon ground red pepper (cayenne)
> 3 to 4 tablespoons reserved garbanzo liquid or water
> Salt
> 2 tablespoons minced parsley

In a blender or food processor, whirl garbanzos, tahini, garlic, lemon juice, and cayenne until smooth. With motor running, add cooking liquid, a little at a time, until mixture has a good dipping consistency. Season to taste with salt. Transfer to a serving bowl. Sprinkle with parsley. Makes 2 cups.

Chutney Cheese Spread

India

"Both cool and fiery with every mouthful" describes this spiced spread. Use our Mango Chutney (page 55) or any other chutney you like. Arrange the appetizer to spread on crackers or triangles of pocket bread, as shown in the photograph on page 19—or, if you prefer, spoon the chutney on top or serve it from a separate bowl.

> ⅓ cup Mango Chutney (page 55, or purchased)
> 1¼ cups drained Milk Cheese (page 64)
> 3 whole cardamom pods, cracked and seeds inside coarsely crushed (discard empty pods)
> ⅛ teaspoon *each* ground ginger, ground nutmeg, and cumin seeds
> 1/16 teaspoon ground red pepper (cayenne)
> Chopped salted pistachios or raisins

Prepare Mango Chutney.

Prepare drained cheese as directed on page 64, but add cardamom, ginger, nutmeg, cumin, and red pepper to the milk with the salt. Shape into a mound; ring or top with chutney. Sprinkle with chopped salted pistachios. Makes 6 to 8 servings.

Holiday Cheese Ball

Sweden

Fond of all its forms and flavors, Scandinavians partake of cheese daily—at simple meals, at festive banquets. Typical for special occasions, this watercress-wreathed and almond-studded cheese ball looks particularly appropriate at Yuletide.

> ⅔ cup finely chopped blanched almonds
> 8 ounces blue-veined cheese, crumbled
> 1 small package (3 oz.) cream cheese, softened
> ½ teaspoon Worcestershire
> 1 to 2 tablespoons whipping cream
> 2 tablespoons minced parsley
> Watercress sprigs

Spread almonds in a shallow pan and toast in a 350° oven for about 8 minutes or until lightly browned. Let cool.

In a food processor or with an electric mixer, blend blue-veined cheese, cream cheese, Worcestershire, and 1 tablespoon of the cream; blend until smooth, adding more cream, if needed. Stir in parsley.

Sprinkle almonds over a large piece of plastic wrap. Shape cheese mixture into a ball and roll in almonds, pressing them into cheese to coat ball well on all sides. Wrap in plastic wrap. Refrigerate for at least 2 hours or until firm. (If made ahead, refrigerate until next day.)

To serve, surround cheese ball with watercress sprigs. Makes a 3½-inch-diameter cheese ball (about 2 cups.)

Pesto Deviled Eggs

Italy

Uova farcite is a delicious way to use freshly made pesto. The bright green basil sauce seasons the egg stuffing with a magnificent garlicky flavor.

> 6 hard-cooked eggs
> 2 tablespoons Pesto (page 55)
> 2 to 3 tablespoons mayonnaise
> Flat-leaf parsley leaves

Halve eggs lengthwise, scoop out yolks, and place them in a small bowl; set aside egg white halves. Add pesto and mayonnaise to yolks and stir until smooth. Spoon mixture into halved egg whites. Garnish each with a parsley leaf. Makes 12 halves.

Chived Egg & Almond Canapés

Norway

Piquant with mustard and chives, these elegant canapés from the far north are garnished in typically Scandinavian fashion—with cucumber slices.

- ½ cup unblanched almonds
- 6 hard-cooked eggs
- 2 tablespoons minced fresh chives or 2 teaspoons freeze-dried chives
- 2 teaspoons Dijon mustard
- ¼ cup *each* sour cream and mayonnaise
  Salt
- 9 to 10 thin slices pumpernickel or rye bread (about 4 inches square)
- 36 to 40 thin cucumber slices

Spread almonds in a shallow pan and toast in a 350° oven for about 8 minutes or until they have a rich, nutlike aroma. Let cool slightly, then whirl in a blender or food processor until powdery (you should have about ⅔ cup ground nuts).

Shred eggs into a medium-size bowl. Add almonds, chives, mustard, sour cream, and mayonnaise; mix until well blended. Season to taste with salt. Spread egg mixture on bread slices; quarter each slice. Top each canapé with a cucumber slice. If made ahead, cover and refrigerate for up to 4 hours. Makes 36 to 40 canapés.

Stuffed Grape Leaves

Greece

Laced with pine nuts and raisins, fragrant with lemon peel and other piquant seasonings, *dolmas* are a popular delicacy from Greece.

- 1 jar (8 oz.) grape leaves, drained, separated, and stems cut off
- 2 tablespoons olive oil
- 1 small onion, finely chopped
- 3 tablespoons minced parsley
- 1 cup short-grain white rice
- ¼ cup pine nuts
- 1 teaspoon dill weed
- ¼ cup chopped raisins
- ½ teaspoon grated lemon peel
  Salt
- 3 cups Root Vegetable Stock or instant vegetable stock (page 33)
- ½ cup olive oil or salad oil
- 6 tablespoons lemon juice

Place grape leaves flat in a large bowl and cover with boiling water. Drain well, pat dry, and set aside.

Heat the 2 tablespoons olive oil in a wide frying pan over medium heat. Add onion and cook until soft but not browned (3 to 5 minutes); stir in parsley, rice, pine nuts, dill, raisins, and lemon peel. Cook, stirring, until nuts are lightly browned (3 to 4 more minutes). Salt lightly and pour in 1½ cups of the stock. Cover, reduce heat, and simmer until liquid is absorbed and rice is almost tender (12 to 15 more minutes). Remove from heat. Mix well.

Spoon about 1 tablespoon filling into the center of each grape leaf, vein side up. Fold in bottom and top ends, then roll from side to side to enclose filling. Place rolls, seam side down, in a large, deep kettle.

After completing one layer, combine the remaining 1½ cups stock, the ½ cup olive oil, and lemon juice in a bowl; pour half of the mixture over stuffed grape leaves.

Assemble the remaining leaves, layer them in kettle and pour the remaining stock mixture over all. Bring to a boil over medium heat, then cover, reduce heat, and simmer until rolls are plump (about 45 minutes). Let cool in cooking liquid. Serve at room temperature. Makes 3 to 4 dozen.

Miso Grilled Mushrooms

Japan

For centuries, miso has been as ordinary as onions in Japanese cooking, but in the West, this fermented, salty soybean paste is less well known than its relative, tofu. Look for the paler type (darker miso is saltier) in Japanese grocery stores.

- 3 tablespoons miso
- ¼ cup sake or dry sherry
- 1 teaspoon grated fresh ginger
- 2 teaspoons honey
- 2 tablespoons lemon juice
- 2 tablespoons white rice vinegar or white (distilled) vinegar
- 1 pound large mushrooms, rinsed and patted dry
- 1 green onion (including top), thinly sliced

In a large bowl, blend miso, sake, ginger, honey, lemon juice, and vinegar. Add mushrooms; stir to coat with marinade, then cover and refrigerate for at least 6 hours or until next day.

Drain marinade into a small pan and set aside. Thread an equal number of mushrooms on each of 8 small skewers, then place them on a lightly greased grill 4 to 6 inches above a solid bed of low-glowing coals. Cook, turning once or twice and brushing occasionally with reserved marinade, until browned on all sides (5 to 10 minutes). Or, to cook indoors, place skewers on a broiler pan and broil about 6 inches from heat, turning as needed and brushing occasionally with reserved marinade, for 6 to 8 minutes. Remove mushrooms from skewers. Heat remaining marinade and serve it in a small bowl, topped with green onions, as a dipping sauce. Serve mushrooms with wooden picks for spearing. Makes about 16 appetizer servings.

Zucchini "Pizza" Hors d'oeuvres

United States

In this American nibble, slices of zucchini—that popular and prolific backyard squash—serve as miniature pizza crusts.

> 4 **medium-size zucchini (about 1½ lbs. *total*)**
> **About 1 cup prepared pizza sauce**
> ⅓ **cup well-drained chopped ripe olives**
> ⅓ **cup thinly sliced green onions (including tops)**
> 1½ **cups (6 oz.) shredded provolone cheese**

Cut zucchini diagonally into ¼-inch-thick slices (about 15 slices from each zucchini). Arrange in a single layer on lightly greased baking sheets. Top each with (in order) 1 to 2 teaspoons pizza sauce (depending on size of zucchini slice), a few olive pieces and green onions, and a sprinkling of cheese. Broil about 6 inches from heat until cheese is melted and lightly browned (4 to 6 minutes). Zucchini should be crisp. Serve hot. Makes about 5 dozen hors d'oeuvres.

Crisp-fried Onions

Denmark   *Pictured on page 30*

Called *stegte løg*, these fragile, crisp, and versatile onions are a favorite snack in Denmark.

> ½ **cup unbleached all-purpose flour**
> 2 **large onions (about 1 lb. *total*), peeled, thinly sliced, and separated into rings**
> **Salad oil**
> **Salt**

Place flour in a bag, add onions, and shake to coat evenly with flour.

Pour oil into a deep 2½ to 3-quart pan to a depth of 1½ inches and heat to 300° on a deep-frying thermometer. Add floured onions, about a fourth at a time, and cook, stirring often, until golden (about 5 minutes). Oil temperature will drop at first but will rise again as onions cook; regulate heat accordingly.

With a slotted spoon, lift out onions and drain on paper towels (discard any scorched onion bits). Serve warm, piled in a napkin-lined basket or in a warmed bowl; sprinkle with salt.

If made ahead, let cool, wrap airtight, and refrigerate for up to 3 days. To reheat, spread onions in a single layer in a shallow rimmed baking sheet. Heat in a 350° oven for 2 to 3 minutes. Makes about 6 cups.

Egg Rolls

China

A Cantonese specialty, these popular little pastry-wrapped packages enclose a savory vegetable filling. Egg roll wrappers are available in many supermarkets in the refrigerated sections—or in Oriental grocery stores.

> **Hot Mustard (recipe follows)**
> 3 **tablespoons salad oil**
> ⅔ **cup thinly sliced green onions (including tops)**
> 2 **cups finely chopped celery**
> ½ **pound mushrooms, finely chopped**
> 2 **large cloves garlic, minced or pressed**
> 3 **tablespoons fresh coriander (cilantro)**
> 4 **teaspoons grated fresh ginger or 1 teaspoon ground ginger**
> 4 **cups bean sprouts**
> 1 **tablespoon *each* soy sauce and dry sherry**
> 1 **teaspoon sugar**
> **Salt**
> 2 **tablespoons salad oil**
> 3 **eggs**
> 1 **tablespoon cornstarch**
> 2 **tablespoons cold water**
> 1 **pound (25 to 30) egg roll wrappers**
> **Salad oil**
> **Catsup**

Prepare Hot Mustard.

Heat the 3 tablespoons oil in a wide frying pan over medium-high heat. Add onions and celery and cook, stirring often, until onions are soft. Stir in mushrooms and cook, stirring, for 3 to 4 more minutes. Then add garlic, coriander, ginger, bean sprouts, soy, sherry, and sugar. Cook, stirring, until mixture is well combined. Remove from heat, season to taste with salt, and set aside.

Heat the 2 tablespoons oil in a 10-inch frying pan over medium-high heat. In a small bowl, lightly beat 2 of the eggs and pour them into pan, tilting to cover bottom. Cook until surface of the egg pancake is dry. With a wide spatula, transfer to a cutting board. With a sharp knife, cut pancake into ¼-inch-wide strips, then cut longer strips into halves or thirds. Add to vegetables. Blend cornstarch and water; add to vegetable mixture. Cook mixture, stirring constantly, over medium heat until thickened. Remove from heat and set aside.

To assemble: Lightly beat the remaining egg. Spoon about 2 rounded tablespoons filling diagonally across each egg roll wrapper about 2 inches above the lower corner. Fold lower corner over filling to cover, then roll over once to enclose filling. Fold over left and right corners, then brush sides and top of remaining corner with egg. Roll up, sealing corner. Place filled egg rolls on a baking sheet, seam side up, and cover with plastic wrap while you fill the remaining wrappers.

At this point, you may wrap egg rolls airtight and refrigerate them for up to 12 hours; freeze for longer storage. Bring to room temperature before cooking.

To cook: Pour oil into a wok or deep pan to a depth of 2 inches and heat to 350° on a deep-frying thermometer. Fry egg rolls, 4 to 6 at a time, turning occasionally, until golden brown on all sides (3 to 4 minutes *total*). Remove with a slotted spoon and drain on paper towels. Keep warm on a baking sheet in a 225° oven while frying remaining rolls.

Serve hot with Hot Mustard and catsup. Makes 25 to 30 egg rolls (for a more convenient size appetizer, cut each roll into 3 equal pieces).

Hot Mustard. Place ¼ cup **dry mustard** in a small bowl. Stirring, slowly pour in ¼ cup cold **water** until smooth. Stir in ⅛ teaspoon **salad oil**. Cover and let stand for 1 hour. Makes about ⅓ cup.

Nachos

Mexico

So delicious that they'll disappear in minutes, *nachos* are simple enough for last-minute preparation—or replenishment.

   12 **six-inch corn tortillas (page 77 or purchased)**
      Salad oil
    1 **pound jack or Münster cheese**
    6 **pickled jalapeño chiles, stemmed and thinly sliced**
      Lime wedges (optional)

Cut each tortilla into 6 wedges. Pour oil into a wok or deep pan to a depth of 1 inch and heat to 350° to 375° on a deep-frying thermometer. Fry tortilla wedges, 6 to 8 at a time, until crisp (1½ to 2 minutes). Drain well on paper towels and let cool.

Meanwhile, cut cheese into ⅛-inch-thick slices, then into 72 one-inch squares.

Arrange tortilla triangles in a single layer on baking sheets and top each with a square of cheese and a slice of chile.

Bake in a 400° oven for 4 to 5 minutes or until cheese is melted. Garnish with lime wedges, if desired; serve immediately. Makes 6 dozen appetizers.

Potato-filled Pastries

India

Offer *samosas*, these popular fried snacks from India, with other delicacies at a party or as a small, savory side dish at dinner. You can assemble the pastries a few hours before serving, but always fry them at the last minute, and serve them hot.

      Samosa Pastry (recipe follows)
    1 **large russet potato (about 10 oz.)**
    2 **tablespoons salad oil**
    ½ **teaspoon black or yellow mustard seeds**
    1 **medium-size onion, finely chopped**
    1 **teaspoon grated fresh ginger or ¼ teaspoon ground ginger**
    ¼ **teaspoon *each* ground coriander, ground cumin, and turmeric**
    ⅔ **cup fresh or frozen peas**
    ½ **teaspoon salt**
    2 **tablespoons water**
      Salad oil

Prepare Samosa Pastry and set aside.

Peel potato and cut it into quarters. Place in small pan and add water to cover. Bring to a boil over high heat, then reduce heat and boil gently, partially covered, until tender (12 to 15 minutes). Drain well, let cool, then cut into ½-inch cubes.

Heat the 2 tablespoons oil in a wide frying pan over medium heat. Add mustard seeds and stir gently until they begin to pop. Add onion, ginger, coriander, cumin, and turmeric. Cook, stirring occasionally, until onions are soft. Mix in potatoes, peas, and salt. Sprinkle with water, cover, reduce heat to very low, and cook until potatoes are soft (6 to 7 minutes). Remove from heat and set aside.

On a floured board, shape dough into a log, then cut it into 24 equal pieces. Flatten one piece and roll into a 3½-inch circle (keep remaining dough covered). Spoon filling over half of circle, and fold other half over filling to form a half-moon. Pinch edges together to seal firmly. Repeat with remaining dough and filling. (At this point, you may cover and refrigerate pastries for 3 to 5 hours. Let them stand at room temperature for 15 minutes before frying.)

Pour oil into a wok or deep pan to a depth of 1 inch and heat to 375° on a deep-frying thermometer. Fry 2 or 3 pastries at a time, carefully turning once, until they are golden brown on both sides (2½ to 3 minutes total). Remove with a slotted spoon and drain on paper towels. Keep hot on a baking sheet in a warm oven (about 225°) while preparing remaining pastries. Makes 2 dozen pastries.

Samosa Pastry. In a medium-size bowl, mix 1½ cups **unbleached all-purpose flour** and ¼ teaspoon **salt.** With a pastry blender or 2 knives, cut in 4 tablespoons **butter** or margarine (cut into small pieces) until mixture resembles coarse crumbs. Stirring with a fork, add 6 to 7 tablespoons cold **water,** a little at a time, until dough becomes stiff.

Turn dough out onto a floured board and knead just until smooth. Shape it into a ball and flatten. Cover with plastic wrap until ready to use.

Spirited Beverages

To infuse your usual cocktail repertoire with a taste of the exotic, here is an international sampler of festive drinks for any occasion.

Sangria, a Spanish favorite for summertime, blends zesty citrus juices with red wine. Our version provides punchbowl quantity.

Toast the first snowfall—or any wintry occasion—with Canada's hot spiced cider. Or cheer holiday guests with cups of mulled wine, fragrant with spices and very British. Surprisingly, Hawaii's contribution is also a heated drink, a ginger and lemon-brightened guava punch. Add 1 to 2 cups of dry white wine, if you like.

Sangria

In a punch bowl, combine 1 gallon **dry red wine,** 2 cups **sugar,** 3 cups **orange juice,** and 1 cup **lemon or lime juice;** stir until sugar dissolves. Add 3 thinly sliced **oranges** and 2 thinly sliced **lemons or limes.** (At this point, you may cover and refrigerate for up to 3 hours.) Serve in tall glasses over **crushed ice.** Use more **lemon or lime slices** to slip over the rim of each glass, if desired. Makes 18 to 20 servings (5 quarts).

Hot Spiced Cider

In a deep 5 to 6-quart kettle, combine 1 gallon **apple cider,** four 2½ to 3-inch **cinnamon sticks,** 24 **whole cloves,** and 1 teaspoon freshly grated **nutmeg.** Bring to a boil over high heat. Cover, reduce heat, and simmer for 25 to 30 minutes. Strain out and discard whole spices. Serve in mugs with a slice of **lemon** and a little **honey.** Makes 16 servings (4 quarts).

Mulled Wine

In a 2-quart pan, combine 2 cups **honey,** 1½ cups **water,** 2 tablespoons **whole cloves,** six 2½ to 3-inch **cinnamon sticks,** and the thin peels, cut into thin strips, of 2 **oranges** and 2 **lemons.** Bring to a boil over medium heat; cover, reduce heat, and simmer for 10 minutes. Discarding whole spices and peel, strain into a deep 6½ to 7-quart kettle; add 2½ cups **lemon juice** and 1 gallon **dry red wine.** Heat, uncovered, over medium heat until steaming (do not boil). Keep warm over very low heat. Serve in mugs, garnishing each portion with a **lemon slice** and a sprinkling of **ground nutmeg.** Makes 18 to 20 servings (5½ quarts).

Hot Spiced Guava Punch

In a 3-quart pan, combine 1 quart **water,** 2 tablespoons **whole cloves,** 2 **whole cinnamon sticks,** and a 1-inch-square slice of **fresh ginger,** cut into thin strips. Bring to a boil over high heat; cover, reduce heat, and boil gently for 10 minutes. Strain, discarding spices; add 1 quart **guava juice** or guava nectar and ½ cup **lemon juice.** Heat until steaming; add ⅓ to ½ cup **sugar** (to taste). Stir well, then serve in mugs and garnish with **lemon twists.** Makes 8 to 10 servings (about 2 quarts).

Onion Tarts

Spain

Called *tortas de cebollas*, these Spanish tarts provide an elegent first course or, in narrow slices, appetizers for a crowd. Pimentos and ripe olives sprinkled through their lattice crusts give them a colorful, festive appearance.

- ⅓ cup olive oil or salad oil
- 3 large onions, thinly sliced
- ¼ teaspoon ground nutmeg
- ½ teaspoon salt
  Tart Shells (recipe follows)
- 3 eggs, lightly beaten
- ¼ cup sliced ripe olives
- 2 to 3 tablespoons sliced pimento

Heat oil in a wide frying pan over medium heat. Add onions, nutmeg, and salt and cook, stirring occasionally, until onions are very soft and lightly browned (30 to 45 minutes). Remove from heat and let cool.

Meanwhile, prepare Tart Shells. Add onions to eggs, then divide mixture evenly between shells. Trim off dough about ½ inch above filling. On a floured board, roll out trimmings, cut them into ¾-inch-wide strips, and weave strips over each tart to make a lattice topping. Fill spaces between lattices with olive and pimento slices. Bake in a 400° oven for 20 to 25 minutes or until pastry is golden. Let cool briefly before cutting into wedges to serve. Makes 2 tarts (24 to 30 appetizers or 12 first course servings).

Tart Shells. In a medium-size bowl, mix 1⅔ cups **unbleached all-purpose flour** and ¼ teaspoon **salt**. With a pastry blender or 2 knives, cut in ½ cup (¼ lb.) firm **butter** or margarine (cut into small pieces) until mixture resembles fine crumbs. Stirring with a fork, add 2 tablespoons **salad oil** (not olive oil), a little at a time; then add 2 to 4 tablespoons very cold **water,** a little at a time, until dough holds together.

Divide dough in half. Shape each portion into a ball, then, on a floured board, roll out each ball to a 12-inch circle. Fit into two 8-inch pie pans.

Carrot-filled Rye Pastries

Finland   *Pictured on page 46*

When they're in the mood for an old-fashioned, country-style dish, Finnish cooks like to serve the filled rye pastries called *piirakka*. Like sandwiches,

the hot, savory bundles make good accompaniments for soup or salad.

  Carrot Filling (recipe follows)
- 1 cup rye flour
- ⅓ cup unbleached all-purpose flour
- ¼ teaspoon salt
- 6 tablespoons butter or margarine, melted and cooled
- 1 egg
- ⅓ cup sour cream
  Egg Butter (recipe follows)

Prepare Carrot Filling.

In a bowl, stir together rye flour, unbleached flour, and salt. Add butter, egg, and sour cream and stir with a fork until well mixed. With lightly floured hands, shape dough into a ball. On a lightly floured board, knead until smooth (2 to 3 minutes). Divide dough into 24 equal pieces, rolling each into a ball. Cover with plastic wrap.

For each pastry, place a ball of dough on a floured board and roll into a circle about 4½ inches in diameter. Spread 2 tablespoons of the filling over dough to within ¾ to ½ inch of edge.

Bring up opposite edges of the circle, pinching sides and ends to form a boat (leaving filling exposed in center). Place pastries slightly apart on a greased baking sheet. Bake in a 350° oven for about 35 minutes or until well browned. If made ahead, let cool on racks; cover and refrigerate until next day. Freeze for longer storage. To reheat, place pastries on a baking sheet and heat, uncovered, in a 350° oven for 8 to 10 minutes (20 minutes if frozen). Prepare Egg Butter and pass it at the table to spread on pastries. Serve pastries hot or warm. Makes 24 pastries.

Carrot Filling. Melt ½ cup (¼ lb.) **butter** or margarine in a wide frying pan over medium heat. Add 6 cups shredded **carrots** (about 12 carrots); 1 large **onion,** finely chopped; and 2 tablespoons **sugar.** Cook, uncovered, stirring often, until carrots are soft and beginning to brown (about 15 minutes). Season to taste with **salt.** Refrigerate until well chilled (2 to 3 hours). Makes about 3 cups.

Egg Butter. In a bowl, finely mash 3 **hard-cooked eggs** with a fork (or force through a wire strainer). Stir in 10 tablespoons (¼ lb. plus 2 tablespoons) **butter** or margarine, softened. Serve at room temperature. If made ahead, cover and refrigerate until next day. Makes about 1 cup.

India's fresh cheese—*creamy, spicy* Chutney Cheese Spread (*page 13*)—*highlights a ring of Mango Chutney (page 55). Catch a taste of pistachio garnish as you spread the cheese, with a little chutney, on accompanying* Chapaties (*page 81*).

Sitter Wanted
for Elderly Ladies
Ellen Oren
784-8987

1322
Home

Salads & Vegetables

From the earth's four corners

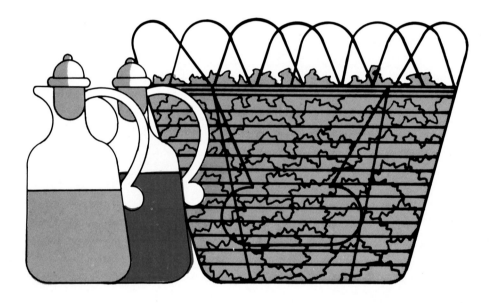

Nibble away to your heart's content—it's virtually impossible to overindulge in the fresh fruit and vegetable feasting offered by this chapter. Grandmother's counsel was wise when she told us to eat abundantly of nature's good greens and yellows (and purple eggplants, ripe red tomatoes, and golden brown potatoes).

Along with their beauty and delicious flavors, fruits and vegetables give us nearly all the vitamins and minerals we need, in low calorie packages of valuable carbohydrates. But since each individual broccoli spear or apple offers only a splash of this with a trace of that, it takes a plentiful variety to attain the full promise of these foods.

Variety will present no problem once this chapter sparks your imagination. For a lift of the spirits after too much plain kale or chard, try the Spinach & Feta Salad, an enticing masterpiece from Greece.

For a change of pace from boiled or baked potatoes, see how marvelously the Tunisians put together potato salad. Or treat yourself and a few guests to Japan's golden Vegetable Tempura.

In all these salads and side dishes, the vitamin and mineral wealth is fragile stuff. Handle produce with care to avoid nutritional loss by too much exposure to air or water. It's a blessing when you can start with freshest possible ingredients from your own garden, but if you can't, shop only for what's in season and looking its fresh, unblemished best. Apart from long-storing roots and bulbs, buy in quantities you can use in a few days; and store, wrapped airtight, in the refrigerator.

Peel and cut fruits and vegetables at the last minute, and only as necessary for cooking speed, eye appeal, or flavor (some peelings are bitter or tough).

Spinach & Feta Salad

Greece

Crumbled, creamy feta—tangy goat cheese of Greek origin—lends spirit to this spinach salad; the whiteness of the cheese contrasts with the dark green leaves. Add mushrooms and rings of sweet red onion, and you've assembled a classical work of art.

1¼ to 1½ pounds spinach
1 medium-size red onion, thinly sliced and separated into rings
½ pound mushrooms, thinly sliced
1 cup (about 6 oz.) crumbled feta cheese
¼ cup lemon juice
½ teaspoon oregano leaves
2 cloves garlic, minced or pressed
¼ teaspoon salt
⅓ cup olive oil
Freshly ground pepper

Remove and discard tough stems and tear large leaves into bite-size pieces. In a large bowl, combine spinach, onion, mushrooms, and cheese.

In a small bowl, mix lemon juice, oregano, garlic, and salt. Drizzle oil over vegetables, tossing to coat spinach, then pour lemon juice mixture over all and mix lightly. Grind pepper over each serving to taste. Serve immediately. Makes 4 to 6 servings.

Celery Root Salad

France

Called *céleri rémoulade,* this exquisite celebration of celery root would traditionally arrive as a first course. It offers a crunchy contrast to delicate Spinach & Cheese Soufflé (page 62) from neighboring Luxembourg.

2 tablespoons lemon juice
2 celery roots (about 1 pound *total*), scrubbed
8 cups boiling salted water
⅓ cup *each* sour cream and mayonnaise
1 egg yolk
1 teaspoon Dijon mustard
2 teaspoons drained capers, finely chopped
2 green onions, thinly sliced (including tops)
1 small clove garlic, minced or pressed
½ teaspoon lemon juice
2 tablespoons finely chopped parsley
Butter lettuce leaves

In a large bowl, combine 8 cups of cold water and the 2 tablespoons lemon juice. Peel celery roots and shred them coarsely. Add to lemon water, mix well, and let stand for about 5 minutes. Drain well. Stir celery root into rapidly boiling salted water for a moment to blanch it; drain well, rinse with cold water to cool it, then drain again.

In a medium-size bowl, blend sour cream and mayonnaise. Beat in egg yolk with a wire whisk. Add mustard, capers, onions, garlic, and the ½ teaspoon lemon juice; blend well. Add drained celery root, mixing lightly to coat well with dressing. Cover and refrigerate until well chilled (at least 3 to 4 hours or until next day).

Sprinkle with parsley and serve on butter lettuce leaves. Makes 4 to 6 servings.

Leek Salad

Wales

According to legend, a 7th century battle was won by the Welsh when they sported leeks in their hats to distinguish themselves from enemy Saxons. Now the leek—the mild-tasting relative of the onion—is the national emblem of Wales and is used in many recipes, such as this salad.

8 medium-size leeks
8 cups boiling salted water
2 hard-cooked eggs, minced
3 tablespoons malt vinegar
2 teaspoons sugar
1 teaspoon dry mustard
1⅓ cups sour cream
Salt and pepper
Butter lettuce leaves
3 tablespoons minced parsley

Trim and discard root ends and tough green tops of leeks; remove all coarse outer leaves. Cut leeks in half lengthwise, then hold each half under cold running water, separating layers to rinse out dirt. Drain well and cut crosswise into ¼-inch-thick slices. Add leeks to boiling salted water; boil gently, uncovered, until just tender (6 to 8 minutes). Drain well and let cool.

Meanwhile, in a small bowl, mix eggs, vinegar, sugar, mustard, and sour cream until well combined. Season to taste with salt and pepper.

Arrange lettuce leaves in a shallow serving dish; top with cooled leeks and spoon dressing over them. Sprinkle with parsley, cover, and refrigerate for 45 minutes to 1½ hours before serving. Makes 4 to 6 servings.

Eggplant & Pepper Salad

Yugoslavia

Ajivar, this Yugoslavian salad, is a definite change of pace from the usual lettuce-based first course. The soft-textured mélange can also double as an appetizer to spread on triangles of pocket bread.

1 large unpeeled eggplant (about 1½ lbs.)
¼ cup olive oil
1 medium-size red or green bell pepper, seeded and diced
2 cloves garlic, minced or pressed
3 tablespoons lemon juice
¼ cup finely chopped parsley
Salt and pepper
Sliced green onions (including tops)
Lettuce leaves (optional)

With a fork, pierce eggplant in several places. Place on a baking sheet; bake, uncovered, in a 400° oven for 40 to 45 minutes or until tender throughout when pierced. Let stand until cool enough to handle, then cut into quarters. Scoop out and dice pulp, discarding skin. Place eggplant in a medium-size bowl and set aside.

Heat oil in a medium-size frying pan over medium heat. Add bell pepper and garlic. Cook, stirring often until almost tender (3 to 4 minutes). Add bell pepper mixture (including oil) to eggplant. Mix in lemon juice and parsley, then season to taste with salt and pepper. Cover and refrigerate for 1 to 3 hours to blend flavors.

Garnish with onions and, if desired, serve on lettuce leaves. Makes 4 to 6 servings.

Tropical Fruit Salad for Two

Polynesia   *Pictured on facing page*

Present this fruited pineapple frigate on a balmy, flower-fragrant summer evening. It overflows with chunks of papaya, mango, and banana, as well as pineapple saved from the hollowed-out shell.

Tropical cargo tempts you to sample its Polynesian splendor from a halved and hollowed pineapple. Besides pineapple chunks, the coconut-sprinkled Tropical Fruit Salad (recipe on this page) offers mango, papaya, banana, and strawberries—all to be drizzled with a tangy papaya-seed dressing.

Coarsely shredded coconut
Papaya-seed Dressing (recipe follows) or juice of 1 lime
1 large pineapple (3½ to 4 lbs.)
1 cup peeled, seeded, diced papaya (1 small papaya; reserve seeds for dressing)
1 large mango (½ to ¾ lb.), peeled, pitted, and diced
1 large banana, cut into ¼-inch-thick slices
1 cup sliced strawberries
½ to 1 cup drained canned lychees

Spread coconut in a shallow pan and toast in a 350° oven for 3 to 5 minutes or until lightly browned. Set aside.

Prepare Papaya-seed Dressing.

Halve pineapple lengthwise through crown. With a curved knife, cut out fruit, leaving a ¼-inch-thick shell. Remove and discard core; dice fruit and place it in a large bowl.

To diced pineapple add papaya, mango, banana, strawberries, and lychees; mix lightly. Spoon fruit into pineapple shells. If made ahead, cover and refrigerate for up to 1 hour. Sprinkle with coconut. Pass dressing at the table to spoon over individual servings. Makes 2 entrée servings.

Papaya-seed Dressing. In a blender or food processor, combine ¼ cup **white wine vinegar;** 1 tablespoon *each* **papaya seeds, minced onion,** and **honey;** ¼ teaspoon **salt;** and ⅛ teaspoon **dry mustard.** Whirl until seeds look like coarsely ground pepper. Add ½ cup **salad oil** and whirl until well blended. Makes about 1 cup.

Watercress Green Salad

Barbados

Thriving in the running streams of the Caribbean islands, watercress adds its distinctive, slightly bitter tang to many a salad of the region.

Lime-Cumin Dressing (recipe follows)
2 large bunches watercress
1 head butter or Boston lettuce
Half of a large red onion
Freshly ground pepper

Prepare Lime-Cumin Dressing.

Remove and discard tough watercress stems; place leaves and small sprigs in a large bowl (you should have 5 to 6 cups). Tear lettuce into bite-size pieces and add to watercress. Thinly slice onion crosswise, then cut slices in half and separate into arcs; add to watercress mixture. Pour dressing over salad and mix lightly. Add pepper to taste. Serve immediately. Makes 6 to 8 servings.

Lime-Cumin Dressing. In a small jar, combine ¼ cup **olive oil,** 2 tablespoons **lime juice,** ¼ teaspoon **sugar,** ½ teaspoon **ground cumin,** ⅛ teaspoon **salt,** and 1 clove **garlic,** minced or pressed. Blend well. If made ahead, let stand at room temperature for up to 8 hours. Shake well before using. Makes about ⅓ cup.

Red Cabbage with Apple

Germany

Like their Slavic and Nordic counterparts, German cooks know dozens of different ways to prepare cabbage. This colorful and vigorous wintertime favorite goes well with Switzerland's Bernese Onion Tart (page 61).

    1 large onion
    2 tablespoons salad oil
    1 medium-size head red cabbage (about 1½ lbs.), shredded
    1 medium-size tart apple, peeled, cored and shredded
    1 large clove garlic, minced or pressed
    1 teaspoon caraway seeds (optional)
    2 tablespoons brown sugar
    ½ cup red wine vinegar
    1 cup water
      Salt

Remove stem and root ends from onion; cut in half lengthwise and thinly slice each half lengthwise so that it falls into slivers.

Heat oil in a wide frying pan (at least 12 inches in diameter) over medium heat; add onion and cook, stirring, until soft. Add cabbage and apple and cook, stirring often, for 5 minutes. Stir in garlic, caraway seeds (if desired), brown sugar, vinegar, and water. Bring to a boil; cover, reduce heat, and simmer, stirring occasionally, until cabbage is very tender and most of the liquid has evaporated (40 to 45 minutes). Season to taste with salt. Makes 4 to 6 servings.

Caraway Potato Salad

Tunisia

Potato salad is such an American favorite that it may come as a surprise that Tunisians enjoy it, too. Try this distinctive version with marinated potatoes and pungent caraway seeds.

    5 medium-size thin-skinned potatoes (about 2 lbs. *total*)
      Boiling salted water
    ½ cup olive oil or salad oil
    ⅓ cup lemon juice
    1 teaspoon *each* caraway seeds and salt
    ½ teaspoon ground cumin
    ⅛ teaspoon ground red pepper (cayenne)
    1 small onion
    1 small green pepper, seeded and cut into thin strips

Scrub potatoes but do not peel; place in a 4-quart pan with boiling salted water to cover. When water returns to a boil, cover, reduce heat, and cook just until tender (25 to 30 minutes).

Drain potatoes and let cool slightly. Cut into ½-inch cubes; place in a large bowl.

In a jar, combine oil, lemon juice, caraway seeds, salt, cumin, and cayenne; blend well. Pour dressing over potatoes and mix lightly. Cover and let stand at room temperature until potatoes are cool (1 to 1½ hours). Meanwhile, remove stem and root ends from onion; cut in half lengthwise and thinly slice each half lengthwise so that it falls into slivers. Add onion and green pepper and mix lightly. Serve at room temperature. Makes 6 servings.

Warm Cole Slaw

Canada

Carrots, onions, and green peppers (as well as invisible vitamin C) brighten up this wintertime salad. Serve it with Thursday Pea Soup (page 36) for a simple supper on a snowy evening.

    4 cups thinly shredded cabbage
    ½ cup finely shredded carrot (1 medium-size)
    ½ cup *each* finely chopped onion and green pepper
    ¼ cup *each* salad oil and cider vinegar
    2 tablespoons sugar
    2 teaspoons dry mustard
    1 teaspoon celery seeds
    ¾ teaspoon salt
    ¼ teaspoon pepper

In a large bowl, combine cabbage, carrot, onion, and green pepper.

In a small pan, combine, oil, vinegar, sugar, mustard, celery seeds, salt, and pepper. Bring to a boil over high heat, stirring until sugar dissolves; continue boiling for 2 minutes. Pour hot dressing over cabbage mixture and mix lightly. Serve immediately. Makes 4 to 6 servings.

Plain & Fancy Oils for Salads & Cooking

Playing an invisible but often quite flavorful role, oils pressed from indigenous nuts, seeds, and fruits distinguish many regional styles of cooking. Olive oil permeates Mediterranean specialties, for example, and sesame oil, in small quantities, seasons many Chinese dishes.

These and more appear today in an array of oils on the shelves of gourmet shops, health food stores, and supermarkets. A few ideas for sampling them are listed below.

Oils stay fresh for many months, if tightly sealed and stored in a cool, dark place. (Olive oil is an exception— we recommend keeping it for only about 2 months.) We don't recommend refrigerating oils, particularly olive oil, because temperature changes oxidize the oil and it will become rancid more rapidly than if left at room temperature. Your best assurance, whatever the oil, is to buy only quantities you'll use up fairly quickly.

Salad or vegetable oils. Pressed from seeds of cotton, corn, peanut, safflower, and sunflower plants, these are the most reasonably priced all-purpose cooking and salad oils. Relatively neutral in flavor, they blend quietly with most vinegars in vinaigrette or mayonnaise.

Corn and peanut oils serve best for stir-frying and deep-frying, since both are able to take high temperatures without smoking. To reuse deep-frying oil, first clarify it by adding pieces of peeled potato to absorb flavors while the oil is still hot. Then, after the oil cools, remove the potato and carefully strain the oil into a jar you can seal. Unlike other oils, deep-frying oil should be refrigerated.

Olive oils. These come in three grades and are favorites because of the flavor they lend, particularly in salad dressings and in sautéing.

Extra-virgin olive oil, finest and most expensive, is available mainly as a gift item in gourmet shops. It comes from the first mechanical pressing of high quality, perfectly ripened olives. Green-gold in hue, rich in fruity ripe-olive flavor, it's most appropriate for dishes in which other ingredients neither clash with nor overwhelm its delicate fragrance. A simple tossed green salad is the perfect foil for extra-virgin olive oil in a vinaigrette made with 3 parts oil to 1 part wine vinegar.

Virgin olive oil, pressed the same way, comes from a slightly less perfect grade of olives, resulting in a lighter color and a flavor that's still quite delicious; you'll see it in gourmet shops and some supermarkets.

Pure olive oil, least expensive and most widely available, comes from a second pressing (with hot water) of the residual pulp from pressing finer grades, combined with a low-grade virgin olive oil. Heat makes it highly acidic; the oil is refined to remove most of this acid and to improve flavor and color.

Nut and sesame oils. Pressed from walnuts, almonds, and hazelnuts, nut oils familiar to French cooks have recently appeared as imports in gourmet shops here. They're best used in salad dressings, where the nut flavor particularly stands out.

Walnut oil, the most delicate of the three, makes delicious vinaigrette (2 to 3 parts oil to 1 part lemon juice or wine vinegar). Spoon either over salad greens or chilled cooked vegetables.

Almond oil, its flavor reminiscent of toasted almonds, is a treat used in vinaigrette, in the same proportions as walnut oil. Or blend some (as little as 2 teaspoons or as much as 3 tablespoons) with 1 cup mayonnaise; then stir in ¼ cup chopped almonds to make a dip for raw vegetables.

Hazelnut oil, most potent of all, is used more sparingly than the first two nut oils. For a dressing over salad greens or slices of apple, pear, orange, or avocado, combine 1 to 2 parts hazelnut oil with 1 part lemon or lime juice. Or blend just a teaspoon of it into 1 cup mayonnaise.

For extra accent to any of these nut-oil dressings, garnish a salad with chopped nuts of the variety from which the oil was pressed.

Sesame oil, also potent and expensive, is pressed from sesame seeds. Chinese cooks use just a dash to season stir-fried vegetables, such as broccoli, snow peas, or bok choy. Look for the oil in Oriental markets if you don't see it in your supermarket.

Vegetable Tempura

Japan   *Pictured on facing page*

Of the world's many deep-fried foods, Japanese tempura, in our opinion, stands apart for its sheer delectable elegance. Inside each fragile shell of our lighter-than-usual batter waits a fresh, crisp vegetable surprise. You should seat guests nearby (don't try to cook for more than four, or you'll never stop) and serve just as soon as the tempura has briefly drained.

> 2 medium-size carrots
> ⅓-pound wedge of a large eggplant
> 1 small green pepper, quartered and seeded
> 12 medium-size mushrooms
> 1 medium-size sweet potato
> 1 medium-size zucchini
> 1 cup broccoli flowerets
> Tempura Dipping Sauce (recipe follows)
> About 6 cups (1½ quarts) salad oil
> Tempura Batter (recipe follows)

Prepare vegetables before you begin cooking (if prepared ahead, cover and refrigerate for up to 3 hours).

Cut carrots crosswise into 4-inch lengths, then cut each piece lengthwise into ¼-inch-thick slices. Slice eggplant into ¼-inch-thick triangular pieces. Cut green pepper into ¼-inch-wide strips. Halve mushrooms through stems. Peel sweet potato and cut in ¼-inch-thick rounds. Cut zucchini diagonally into ¼-inch-thick slices. Trim stems of flowerets to ¾ inch.

Prepare Dipping Sauce. Divide it equally among 4 individual serving bowls. Pour oil into a wok or deep pan to a depth of 1½ to 2 inches and heat to 375° on a deep-frying thermometer. Meanwhile, prepare Tempura Batter.

To cook tempura, dip each vegetable piece into batter with chopsticks or tongs; let excess drip off, then gently lower into hot oil. Cook several pieces at a time without crowding, turning occasionally, until crisp and golden (2 to 3 minutes). Drain briefly on a wire rack set on a shallow pan. Serve immediately. Frequently skim off and discard any bits of batter from the oil as you continue frying.

Let guests dip each piece into sauce. Makes 4 servings.

Tempura Dipping Sauce. In a small pan, combine 1 cup **instant vegetable stock** (page 33) and ¼ cup *each* **soy sauce** and **dry sherry.** Bring to a boil over high heat, then remove from heat and let cool to room temperature. Finely shred enough **fresh ginger** and **daikon radish** to make about 3 tablespoons *each.* Pass ginger and radish at the table to add to individual bowls of sauce. Makes 1½ cups.

Tempura Batter. In a small bowl, lightly beat 1 cup **ice-cold water,** 1 **egg,** and ¼ teaspoon *each* **baking soda** and **salt.** Add 1 cup **cake flour** (unsifted); mix just until blended (batter will be lumpy). Sprinkle ⅓ cup more **cake flour** (unsifted) over top of batter. With a fork, stir batter one or two strokes (do not blend thoroughly—most of the last addition of flour should be floating on top of the batter). Fill a larger bowl half full of ice; set the batter bowl in it to keep cold while you cook.

Daikon Radish & Carrot Salad

Japan   *Pictured on facing page*

Though its colorful carrots seem to steal the show, this fragrant salad, called *daikon namasu,* also celebrates Japan's enormous white daikon radish. Traditionally served in small decorative bowls, it provides a bright and bold-flavored contrast to brown rice or any other grain dish.

> 1 large daikon radish (about 1½ pounds) or 1½ pounds small turnips
> 1 large carrot
> ¼ cup thinly sliced green onions (white part only)
> ½ cup white rice vinegar or white (distilled) vinegar
> 4 teaspoons soy sauce
> 2 teaspoons sugar
> ½ teaspoon grated fresh ginger
> Watercress sprigs

Peel daikon and carrot; cut into julienne strips about 1 inch long, or shred coarsely. In a large bowl, combine daikon, carrot, and onions.

In a small bowl, mix vinegar, soy, sugar, and ginger; stir until sugar dissolves. Combine with daikon mixture, mixing lightly. Cover and refrigerate for 1 to 3 hours to blend flavors. Serve garnished with watercress sprigs. Makes 6 to 8 servings.

Its every bite a surprise, *golden crisp Vegetable Tempura (recipe on this page) ranks among our most popular culinary imports from Japan. We've used a light-as-air batter coating for the vegetables. The tempura and its dipping sauce share the menu with Daikon Radish & Carrot Salad (also on this page) and sesame-sprinkled brown rice.*

Soups & Stews

Meals-in-a-bowl from the world's cuisines

Cooked all over the world (usually for hours of slow simmering), both soups and stews traditionally are made with a little of this, a little of that, depending on what's at hand in the kitchen. The result may be spontaneous and unpredictable—as the cook keeps tasting, guessing, and enhancing.

There's precious little difference between soup and stew, except for the amount of liquid. And even this distinction is elusive, as some soups are very thick (often with cream), while some stews are definitely soupy. Then again, some stews are simmered in a broth that is later served up as soup.

Thick or thin, soup or stew, what really counts is that both lend comfort, heartiness, and pleasing informality as few other dishes can. It's almost impossible, for one thing, to duplicate the slow blending and mellowing of flavors that happen in a soup or stew. And in a vegetarian diet, which lacks the bulk provided by meat, the robust flavors and substance of soups and stews are particularly satisfying.

In this chapter, we offer quite a varied selection of choice soups and stews from around the world. Many are hot and hearty for wintry weather; some, like the light and lyrical French *ratatouille,* are served at room temperature—or even chilled, for summer refreshment.

Soups and stews seem somehow to require crusty bread alongside. Here and there, we suggest loaves from our "Breads" chapter (pages 80–87) to enhance a specific soup or stew. But it's likely to be more fun to experiment on your own with choices not only of bread, but of other accompaniments as well. For guidance on complementary protein matching, consult the chart on page 7.

Clear Broth with Vegetables

Belgium

In this artistic creation of Belgian chefs' "nouvelle cuisine," fresh vegetables glisten like gems in a clear, golden broth. Light in calories, *soupe aux petits légumes nouveaux* is also rich in vitamins.

- 3 medium-size slender zucchini (about ¾ lb. *total*)
- 4 medium-size slender carrots
- 1 medium-size turnip (about 6 oz.)
- 3 tablespoons butter or margarine
- 4 cups instant vegetable stock (page 33)
- ¼ cup thinly sliced green onions (including tops)
  Salt and white pepper
  Italian (flat-leaf) parsley

Cut zucchini lengthwise into quarters; thinly slice crosswise to make triangular pieces; set aside. Repeat with carrots. Cut turnip into 8 equal wedges; slice crosswise into triangular pieces about the same size as zucchini and carrot pieces.

Melt butter in a 3-quart pan over medium low heat. Stir in carrots and turnips and cook, uncovered, stirring often, until tender-crisp (5 to 7 minutes). Add stock and bring to a boil over high heat. Stir in zucchini and onions. Cover, reduce heat, and simmer just until zucchini is tender-crisp (2 to 3 minutes). Season to taste with salt and pepper. Garnish each serving with a parsley sprig. Makes 6 to 7 cups.

Poached Egg-Garlic Soup

Spain

Gloriously garlicky, this hearty soup celebrates the Mediterranean region's popular little flavor-bursting bulb. As you toast the croutons with garlic, be sure to keep the heat medium-low to prevent the garlic from burning and turning bitter.

- 4 slices firm white bread
- 1 tablespoon butter or margarine
- 1 tablespoon olive oil
- 4 cloves garlic, minced or pressed
- 4 cups Root Vegetable Stock or instant vegetable stock (page 33)
- 1 bay leaf
- 1 teaspoon lemon juice
- 4 eggs
  Finely chopped parsley or coarsely chopped fresh coriander (cilantro)

Trim crusts from bread and save for other uses; cut bread into ½-inch cubes. Heat butter and oil in a wide, deep frying pan over medium-low heat. Add bread cubes and garlic and cook, stirring often, until bread is crisp and lightly browned. Remove from pan and keep warm.

Combine stock, bay leaf, and lemon juice in pan. Bring to a simmer over medium heat. Break one of the eggs into a saucer and carefully slip it into hot broth; repeat with remaining eggs. Poach eggs until whites are set but yolks are still liquid (about 4 minutes).

With a slotted spoon, carefully transfer each egg to a warm soup bowl. Ladle broth over eggs and sprinkle each serving with croutons and parsley. Makes about 6 cups.

Shiitake Egg Drop Soup

Orient

Most familiar in dried, imported form, *shiitake* (a type of dark brown mushroom) are nowadays cultivated in the United States, as well as in their native forests of the Far East. Since they're extraordinarily rich in protein, iron, calcium, and phosphorus, it's not surprising that Orientals consider them an elixir of life, bestowing youthful vigor. Look for dried shiitake in Oriental food markets.

- 1 ounce dried shiitake mushrooms
- 3 cups Root Vegetable Stock or instant vegetable stock (page 33)
- 2 teaspoons soy sauce
- ½ teaspoon grated fresh ginger or ⅛ teaspoon ground ginger
- 2 tablespoons *each* cornstarch and water
- 1 egg
- 3 tablespoons thinly sliced green onions (including tops)
  White pepper

Place mushrooms in a bowl, pour in warm water to cover, and let soak for about 30 minutes. With a slotted spoon, lift out mushrooms, reserving 1 cup of the liquid. Blot mushrooms dry with paper towels and cut into ¼-inch-wide strips.

In a 2-quart pan, combine stock and reserved liquid. Stir in soy, ginger, and mushrooms. Stir together cornstarch and water and add to soup. Bring to a boil over high heat, stirring constantly. Beat egg lightly and stir into boiling soup. Remove from heat and continue stirring until egg separates into shreds. Sprinkle with onions and season to taste with pepper. Serve immediately. Makes about 5 cups.

Chunky Gazpacho

Spain, Mexico

Though we think of it as a Mexican soup, *gazpacho* actually began in an Andalusian kitchen in southern Spain. An abundance of garden-crisp vegetables makes the chilled soup a refreshing as well as beautiful meal opener or warm-weather entrée. Made up to 3 days in advance, it offers carefree elegance with cheese and a loaf of good bread. For a thinner version, stir in up to 1 cup tomato juice.

- 1 large can (28 oz.) stewed tomatoes
- 1 medium-size green pepper, seeded and finely chopped
- ½ cup *each* thinly sliced green onions (including tops) and finely diced celery
- ¼ cup *each* chopped watercress and sliced pimento-stuffed green olives
- 2 cloves garlic, minced or pressed
- ¼ cup finely chopped parsley
- 3 tablespoons olive oil or salad oil
- 1 tablespoon red wine vinegar
- 1 teaspoon soy sauce
  Salt and pepper
  Grated Parmesan cheese

In a bowl, combine tomatoes (break up with a spoon) and their liquid, green pepper, onions, celery, watercress, olives, garlic, parsley, oil, vinegar, and soy; stir well. Cover and refrigerate until next day or as long as 3 days. Season to taste with salt and pepper. Pass Parmesan cheese to sprinkle over individual servings. Makes about 5 cups.

Cucumber Walnut Soup

Bulgaria

Too mountainous for extensive agriculture, Bulgaria is blessed with a fertile valley of summer sunshine known as its "California." *Tarator*, a tangy-crunchy chilled soup from this region, combines cucumbers with walnuts to refresh a warm evening anywhere. Round out an international menu with Bulgur & Mint Salad (page 41).

- 1 large cucumber (about 1 lb.), peeled and seeded
- 2½ cups plain yogurt
- ½ cup finely chopped walnuts
- 1 tablespoon minced fresh dill or 1 teaspoon dill weed
- 1 large clove garlic, minced or pressed
- 2 tablespoons salad oil
  Salt

Shred enough of the cucumber to make ¼ cup; set aside. Coarsely chop remaining cucumber and place in a blender or food processor. Add yogurt and whirl until smooth. Transfer mixture to a bowl and mix in reserved cucumber, walnuts, dill, garlic, and oil. Season to taste with salt. Cover and refrigerate until cold (at least 1 hour). Stir well.

Serve in chilled bowls. Makes about 4 cups.

Rich Potato-Leek Soup

Denmark   *Pictured on facing page*

Commonplace on Danish dinner tables, this easy and rich-tasting soup tingles with the typically Scandinavian vigor of dill weed and sour cream. Rye Bread (page 85) contrasts pleasingly with the light green soup. Round out supper with spicy Lentil Salad (page 48).

- 4 large leeks (2 to 2½ lbs. *total*)
- 2 tablespoons butter or margarine
- 1 tablespoon dill weed
- 4 large potatoes (2½ to 3 lbs *total*), peeled and sliced
  About ½ teaspoon salt
- ⅛ teaspoon white pepper
- 3 cups Root Vegetable Stock or instant vegetable stock (page 33)
- 2 cups milk
  Sour cream
  Dill sprigs

Trim and discard root ends and tough green tops of leeks; remove all coarse outer leaves. Cut leeks in half lengthwise, then hold each one under cold running water, separating layers to rinse out dirt. Cut into thin slices.

Melt butter in a 5-quart kettle over medium heat. Add leeks and dill; cook, stirring often, until leeks are soft. Add potatoes, ½ teaspoon salt, pepper, and stock. Bring to a boil over high heat; cover, reduce heat, and simmer until potatoes are tender (30 to 40 minutes).

In blender or food processor, whirl soup, a portion at a time, until smooth. Return purée to kettle

Soothe away winter's chill with a steaming bowl of Rich Potato-Leek Soup from Denmark (recipe on this page). Make a meal of it with Crisp-fried Onions (page 15), a loaf of robust Rye Bread (page 85), slabs of fontina and Havarti cheeses, and Danish beer.

and stir in milk. Cook over medium heat, stirring often, until soup is steaming. Add more salt, if needed. Top each serving with a dollop of sour cream and dill sprigs. Makes about 10 cups.

Carrot & Rice Soup

Norway

After skiing home from school on a sunless, snowy afternoon, Norwegian children might warm up in the kitchen by dunking freshly baked bread into bowls of this colorful carroty soup. Though it doesn't typically appear on a Norwegian winter menu, a crisp garden salad makes a tasty accompaniment.

    Sliced almonds
3 tablespoons butter or margarine
3 large carrots (about 1 lb. *total*), chopped
2 large stalks celery, chopped
1 small onion, chopped
    About ½ teaspoon salt
⅛ teaspoon *each* white pepper and ground nutmeg
4 cups Root Vegetable Stock or instant vegetable stock (page 33)
2 cups cooked brown rice (page 45)
½ pint (1 cup) half-and-half (light cream)

Spread almonds in a shallow pan and toast in a 350° oven for about 8 minutes or until lightly browned.

Melt butter in a 3-quart pan over medium heat. Add carrots, celery, and onion and cook, stirring, until onion is soft but not browned. Mix in ½ teaspoon salt, pepper, and nutmeg; then add 2 cups of the stock and bring to a boil over high heat. Cover, reduce heat, and simmer until carrots are tender (about 10 minutes).

In a blender or food processor, whirl soup until smooth. Return purée to pan and add rice and remaining 2 cups stock. Bring to a boil over high heat; cover, reduce heat, and simmer for 5 minutes. Stir in half-and-half; add more salt, if needed. Sprinkle each serving with almonds. Makes about 7 cups.

Zesty Tomato Soup with Orange

The Caribbean

Carrots, tomatoes, and orange juice brighten this blender-smooth soup from the Caribbean. Zesty with flavor, low in calories, it's a refreshing choice for a summer evening. Or try it for lunch, with Watercress Green Salad (page 23) and Whole Wheat Baguettes (page 83).

1 tablespoon butter or margarine
1 medium-size onion, chopped
5 medium-size tomatoes (about 2 lbs *total*), cored and chopped
1 medium-size carrot, chopped
1 teaspoon *each* dry basil and sugar
2 instant vegetable stock base cubes or 2 teaspoons instant vegetable stock base granules (page 33)
1 cup orange juice
    Salt and pepper
1 whole orange, thinly sliced (optional)

Melt butter in a 3-quart pan over medium heat; add onion and cook until soft. Stir in tomatoes, carrot, basil, sugar, and stock base cubes. Bring to a boil over high heat; cover, reduce heat, and simmer, stirring often, until carrot is tender (15 to 20 minutes).

In a blender or food processor, whirl soup, a portion at a time, until smooth. Return purée to pan and add orange juice. Cook over medium heat, stirring occasionally, until soup is steaming. Season to taste with salt and pepper. Serve with orange slices on top, if desired. Makes about 5 cups.

Yogurt Soup with Barley & Spinach

Armenia

In Middle Eastern kitchens, yogurt is a staple used virtually every day, mostly in sauces. But this hot soup shows off yogurt's versatility in a more unusual and quite delicious fashion. To its rich milk nourishment, barley and spinach add their special vigor.

7 cups Root Vegetable Stock or instant vegetable stock (page 33)
½ cup pearl barley, rinsed and drained
1 pound spinach or 1 package (10 oz.) frozen leaf spinach
3 tablespoons *each* cornstarch and water
1 pint (2 cups) plain yogurt
2 teaspoons sugar
4 tablespoons butter or margarine
1 medium-size onion, finely chopped
2 cloves garlic, minced or pressed
2 tablespoons finely chopped fresh mint or 4 teaspoons crushed dry mint
    Salt and pepper

(Continued on page 34)

Soup Stock: Source of Flavor

In traditional kitchens around the world, soup stock usually comes together with whatever scraps the cook happens to have on hand. A liquid base to which more obvious ingredients are added later, stock is the heart of the soup's flavor.

Our two stocks are judiciously seasoned to sing with good flavor. Root Vegetable Stock is flavored with vegetables available the year around. Green Vegetable Stock is made with greens of the season. Unless one of the stocks is called for by name in a recipe, the two can be used interchangeably.

Stock making takes time (two hours or so) but you can always simmer a huge potful one afternoon, then freeze labeled portions for later use.

Instant vegetable stock. If you're in a hurry, you can always use instant vegetable stock base (labeled as vegetable-flavored instant bouillon or vegetarian-style instant bouillon) instead. For each cup of vegetable stock called for in a recipe, substitute 1 cube or 1 teaspoon granules per cup of boiling water. *Be sure to taste the soup before adding salt* when using instant vegetable stock base. You may not need any additional salt.

Root Vegetable Stock

     2 tablespoons butter or margarine
     3 large carrots, coarsely chopped
     1 large turnip, coarsely chopped
     2 large stalks celery, thinly sliced (include leaves, if any)
     2 large onions, chopped
    12 cups water
     2 teaspoons salt
     6 large parsley sprigs
    ½ bay leaf
     1 teaspoon thyme leaves
     2 whole cloves garlic (optional)
    ¼ teaspoon black peppercorns (optional)

Melt butter in a 7 to 8-quart kettle over medium-high heat. Add carrots, turnip, celery, and onions. Cook, stirring occasionally, until vegetables are golden (about 15 minutes).

Stir in water, salt, parsley, bay leaf, and thyme. If desired, add garlic and peppercorns. Bring to a boil over high heat. Cover, reduce heat, and simmer for 1½ hours. Strain and discard vegetables. To freeze, let broth cool and pour into freezer containers. Makes about 10 cups.

Green Vegetable Stock

This stock is best made with two different greens— 4 cups of each. Choose from spinach, Swiss chard, kale, or mustard greens; the latter two make a stronger-flavored stock.

     8 cups coarsely shredded, lightly packed greens (see above)
     1 small head green cabbage, coarsely shredded
     1 cup lightly packed parsley sprigs
     2 large stalks celery, chopped (include leaves, if any)
     1 large onion, coarsely chopped, or 2 leeks, sliced (include lower third of green tops)
     3 large cloves garlic, minced or pressed
     2 teaspoons salt
     1 teaspoon thyme leaves
     1 bay leaf
    ½ teaspoon black peppercorns
    12 cups water

In a 7 to 8-quart enamel or stainless steel kettle, combine greens, cabbage, parsley, celery, onion, garlic, salt, thyme, bay leaf, peppercorns, and water. Bring to a boil over high heat. Reduce heat and simmer, uncovered, for 1½ hours.

Strain and discard vegetables. To freeze, let broth cool and pour into freezer containers. Makes about 8 cups.

In a 4 to 5-quart kettle, bring stock to a boil over high heat; add barley. Cover, reduce heat to medium-low, and cook until barley is tender (about 1 hour).

Meanwhile, remove and discard tough spinach stems; cut leaves crosswise into ½-inch-wide strips (or partially defrost frozen spinach, cut into strips, then drain well).

In a small pan, blend cornstarch and water until smooth, then stir in yogurt and sugar. Cook, stirring often, over medium-low heat until mixture boils. Remove from heat and set aside.

Melt butter in a small frying pan over medium heat. Add onion and garlic, and cook, stirring, until onion is soft but not browned. Stir in mint, remove from heat, and set aside.

When barley is tender, add spinach and continue simmering for 3 more minutes. Stir in yogurt mixture and bring to a boil over high heat; cook, stirring, for 3 more minutes. Thin with more stock or water, if needed; season to taste with salt and pepper.

Serve with onion butter on top. Makes about 12 cups.

Cabbage Soup with Caraway

Finland

Like few other vegetables, compact, sturdy-leafed green cabbage has obliged northern Europe by holding onto its vitamin-C-laden goodness through long, freezing winters. Here, the king of the cole family marries another Scandinavian staple—milk—in a comfortingly creamy Finnish soup. Enjoy it with grilled cheese sandwiches on Rye Bread (page 85).

> 3 tablespoons butter or margarine
> 1 medium-size onion, finely chopped
> ¼ teaspoon caraway seeds
> 1 medium-size head green cabbage (1½ to 2 lbs.), cored and coarsely shredded
> 1½ cups Root Vegetable Stock or instant vegetable stock (page 33)
> 1 cup milk
> 1½ cups half-and-half (light cream)
> Salt and white pepper

Melt butter in a 3 to 4-quart pan over medium heat. Add onion and caraway seeds; cook, stirring occasionally, until onion is soft. Mix in cabbage and cook, stirring occasionally, until limp (about 3 minutes). Pour in stock and bring to a boil over high heat. Reduce heat and simmer, uncovered, for 15 minutes.

In a blender or food processor, whirl about half of the mixture until smooth. Return purée to pan and add milk and half-and-half. Cook over medium heat, stirring often, until soup is steaming but not boiling. Season to taste with salt and pepper. Makes about 7 cups.

Golden Tofu-Cauliflower Soup

Thailand

Asia's protein-packed tofu—known as "meat of the fields"—lends its creamy presence to countless concoctions of the Far East. Inspired by a Thai recipe, this quick and easy tofu-blended soup tingles the senses as it satisfies. It teams up deliciously with Spinach & Feta Salad (page 21) and hot, chewy Chapaties (page 81).

> 2 tablespoons salad oil
> 1 medium-size onion, sliced
> 2 cloves garlic, minced or pressed
> 1 teaspoon curry powder
> 2 teaspoons *each* ground coriander and ground cumin
> 4 cups Root Vegetable Stock, Green Vegetable Stock, or instant vegetable stock (page 33)
> 2 cups coarsely chopped cauliflower
> ½ pound medium-firm tofu, cubed
> 1 teaspoon salt
> 3 tablespoons lemon juice
> 2 tablespoons minced parsley

Heat oil in a 4-quart pan over medium heat. Add onion and cook, stirring occasionally, until soft. Stir in garlic, curry powder, coriander, and cumin and cook, stirring, for 1 more minute. Add stock, cauliflower, tofu, and salt. Bring to a boil over high heat; cover, reduce heat, and simmer until cauliflower is tender (about 8 minutes).

In a blender or food processor, whirl soup, a portion at a time, until smooth. Return purée to pan and add lemon juice. Cook over medium heat, stirring often, until soup is steaming. Garnish with parsley. Makes 6 cups.

Vigoroso *best describes the flavor of Winter Minestrone (page 37), sprinkled with jack cheese. And the perfect bread to go with it? Garlic Cheese Bread (page 85)—the Italians call it* focaccia.

Thursday Pea Soup

Sweden

Since the Middle Ages, when Sweden was Roman Catholic and Thursdays were meatless, thick pea soup has been a Thursday night tradition. This version uses either yellow split peas or the more familiar green ones.

    1 pound (about 2⅓ cups) yellow or green
       split peas
    2 tablespoons butter or margarine
    2 medium-size onions, finely chopped
    2 large carrots, finely chopped
    1 small rutabaga, peeled and diced
    ½ teaspoon *each* cumin seeds and
       marjoram leaves
    ¼ teaspoon white pepper
    7 cups Root Vegetable Stock or
       instant vegetable stock (page 33)
    3 tablespoons cider vinegar
       Salt

Rinse peas and sort through, discarding any foreign material. Drain well.

Melt butter in a 4 to 5-quart kettle over medium heat; add onions, carrots, rutabaga, cumin, marjoram, and pepper. Cook, stirring often until onions are soft but not browned. Add peas and stock and bring to a boil over high heat. Cover, reduce heat, and simmer, stirring occasionally to prevent sticking, until peas lose their shape (2 to 2½ hours). Mix in vinegar; add salt, if needed. Makes 10 to 12 cups.

Creamy Onion Soup

Germany

Bad Dürkheim in the Rhine Valley is the home of this inviting soup called *Pfälzer Zwiebelsuppe.* Served with one of the dry Rieslings of the area, it makes a cheerful repast.

       Rye Croutons (recipe follows)
    3 medium-size onions
    4 tablespoons butter or margarine
    ½ teaspoon caraway seeds
    ¼ teaspoon thyme leaves
    1 tablespoon unbleached all-purpose flour
    2 cups Root Vegetable Stock or
       instant vegetable stock (page 33)
    ¾ cup half-and-half (light cream) or milk
       Salt and white pepper

Prepare Rye Croutons; set aside.

Remove stem and root ends from onions; cut in half lengthwise and thinly slice each half lengthwise so that it falls into slivers. Melt butter in a 2 to 3-quart pan over medium heat. Add onions and cook, stirring occasionally, until soft but not browned (about 15 minutes). Mix in caraway seeds and thyme, then stir in flour to coat onions. Stirring constantly, slowly pour in stock and bring to a boil. Cover, reduce heat, and simmer for 15 minutes.

In a blender or food processor, whirl about half of the onions and a little broth until smooth. Return purée to pan and stir in half-and-half. Cook over medium heat, stirring occasionally, until soup is steaming. Season to taste with salt and pepper. Top each serving with croutons. Makes about 4 cups.

Rye Croutons. Trim crusts from 3 slices **rye bread** (save crusts for other uses, if desired). Cut bread into ½-inch cubes; set aside. Heat 1 tablespoon **salad oil** and 1 tablespoon **butter** or margarine in a wide frying pan over medium heat. Mix in 1 small clove **garlic,** minced or pressed. Add bread cubes and stir until coated with butter mixture. Spread in a single layer on a baking sheet. Bake in a 325° oven for 15 to 20 minutes or until crisp and well browned. Makes about 1 cup.

Avocado Soup with Condiments

Mexico

An array of colorful condiments dresses up this full-meal Mexican vegetable soup. Most of the condiments are cold and easily assembled in advance. But heat the tortilla chips before serving—then, when you drop them into the soup, they'll sizzle!

    1 large onion
    2 tablespoons olive oil or salad oil
    2 cloves garlic, minced or pressed
    ½ teaspoon oregano leaves
    6 cups Root Vegetable Stock or
       instant vegetable stock (page 33)
    1 can (16 oz.) tomatoes
    2 medium-size carrots, thinly sliced
    2 medium-size red potatoes, scrubbed
       and diced
    1 teaspoon *each* sugar and salt
    ¼ teaspoon pepper
    2 medium-size ripe avocados
       Lime or lemon juice
    2 cups (8 oz.) *each* shredded jack cheese
       and Cheddar cheese
       Condiments (suggestions follow)

Remove stem and root ends from onion; cut in half lengthwise and thinly slice each half lengthwise so that it falls into slivers.

Heat oil in a 5 to 6-quart kettle over medium heat. Add onion, garlic, and oregano; cook, stirring occasionally, until onion is soft (8 to 10 minutes). Mix in stock, tomatoes (break up with a spoon) and their liquid, carrots, potatoes, sugar, salt, and pepper. Bring to a boil over high heat; cover, reduce heat, and simmer until potatoes are tender (about 25 minutes).

Meanwhile, halve avocados lengthwise and remove pits; peel, cut into thin slices, and place in a bowl. Mix slices lightly with lime juice to prevent darkening.

To serve, line soup bowls with cheese and avocado slices and ladle soup over. Pass condiments at the table. Makes 10 to 12 cups.

Condiments. Choose from **sour cream,** thinly sliced **green onions** (including tops), chopped **hard-cooked eggs,** hot **tortilla chips** (heat in a 350° oven for 8 to 10 minutes), and **bottled green taco sauce.**

Winter Minestrone

Italy   *Pictured on page 35*

Sharing the board with hot Italian Garlic Cheese Bread (page 85), here's sustenance to sate the most ravenous winter hunger. A glance through its list of robust ingredients shows why "minestrone" translates as "big soup." Pass around a bowl of shredded jack cheese to sprinkle atop each serving.

   3 tablespoons olive oil
   1 large onion, finely chopped
   1 large stalk celery, finely chopped
   2 large cloves garlic, minced or pressed
   1 teaspoon dry basil
   ½ teaspoon *each* dry rosemary, oregano leaves, and thyme leaves
   ¼ cup pearl barley
   2 medium-size thin-skinned potatoes, diced
   2 large carrots, diced
   8 cups Root Vegetable Stock or instant vegetable stock (page 33)
   1 large turnip, peeled and diced
   1 can (about 15 oz.) red kidney beans or white kidney beans (*cannellini*)
   ⅔ cup small shell macaroni or elbow macaroni
   ¼ cup tomato paste
   2 cups finely shredded green cabbage
     Salt and pepper
   1½ cups (6 oz.) shredded jack cheese

Heat oil in a 5-quart kettle over medium heat; add onion, celery, garlic, basil, rosemary, oregano, and thyme; cook, stirring, until onion is soft. Add barley, potatoes, carrots, and stock and bring to a boil over high heat. Cover, reduce heat, and simmer for 20 minutes. Add turnip. Cover and continue simmering for 20 more minutes.

Mix in beans and their liquid, macaroni, and tomato paste. Bring to a boil over high heat; cover, reduce heat, and boil gently until macaroni is tender (about 15 minutes). Then add cabbage and cook, uncovered, until cabbage is tender-crisp (about 5 more minutes).

Season to taste with salt and pepper. Pass cheese to sprinkle over individual servings. Makes 12 to 14 cups.

Black Bean & Rice Soup

Jamaica   *Pictured on page 38*

Throughout the Caribbean, and Latin America, the humble black bean has held body and soul together for many a generation. In this Jamaican soup, beans combine with rice for complete protein.

   1 pound (about 2½ cups) dried black beans
   6 cups water
   4 cups Root Vegetable Stock or instant vegetable stock (page 33)
   ¼ cup olive oil
   1 large onion, finely chopped
   4 to 6 cloves garlic, minced or pressed
   1½ teaspoons *each* ground cumin and oregano leaves
     About 2 teaspoons salt
   1½ cups cooked brown rice (page 45)
   2 to 3 tablespoons red wine vinegar
   2 cups sour cream
   4 green onions (including tops), thinly sliced
   6 radishes, thinly sliced
     Lime or lemon wedges

Rinse beans and sort through, discarding any foreign material. Drain well. Place beans and water in a 4 to 5-quart kettle and bring to a boil over high heat. Cover, reduce heat, and simmer until beans swell and absorb most of the water (30 to 45 minutes). Add stock and continue simmering, covered, until beans are tender (about 1 more hour).

Meanwhile, heat oil in an 8-inch frying pan over medium heat. Add onion, garlic, cumin, and oregano and cook, stirring, until onion is soft. Set aside.

In a blender or food processor, whirl about 2 cups of the beans and a little broth until smooth;

(Continued on page 39)

return purée to kettle. Stir in 2 teaspoons salt, onion mixture, rice, and vinegar. Cook over medium heat until soup is steaming. Add more salt, if needed. Pass sour cream, green onions, radishes, and lime wedges at the table. Makes 14 to 16 cups.

Mediterranean Lentil-Eggplant Stew

Sicily

This Sicilian stew from the lentil's native Mediterranean land makes a hearty meal-in-a-bowl.

        1 large onion
        6 tablespoons olive oil
        3 cloves garlic, minced or pressed
        1 large stalk celery, thinly sliced
        1 large carrot, thinly sliced
        ¼ cup chopped parsley
        1 teaspoon *each* dry basil and oregano leaves
        1 package (12 oz.) lentils
        2 cups water
        2 cups Green Vegetables Stock or instant vegetable stock (page 33)
        1 medium-size eggplant (1 to 1½ lbs.), unpeeled, cut into ½-inch cubes
        1 can (6 oz.) tomato paste
        ¼ cup red wine vinegar
        ¼ teaspoon ground cinnamon
          About ½ teaspoon salt
        ⅛ teaspoon pepper
          Chopped parsley
          Shredded jack cheese

Remove stem and root ends from onion; cut in half lengthwise and cut each half lengthwise so that onion falls into slivers. Heat 2 tablespoons of the oil in a 4 to 5-quart kettle over medium heat. Add onion and cook, stirring, until soft. Stir in garlic, celery, carrot, the ¼ cup parsley, basil, oregano, lentils, water, and stock. Bring to a boil over high heat; cover, reduce heat, and simmer for 1 hour.

Meanwhile, heat 2 tablespoons of the remaining oil in a wide nonstick frying pan over medium heat. Add half of the eggplant and cook, stirring frequently, until lightly browned and beginning to

soften (10 to 15 minutes). Remove and set aside. Repeat with remaining oil and eggplant.

After lentil mixture has simmered for 1 hour, stir in browned eggplant, tomato paste, vinegar, cinnamon, ½ teaspoon salt, and pepper. Continue simmering, covered, until vegetables are tender (about 1 more hour), adding up to 1 cup more water during cooking if stew begins to stick. Add more salt, if needed.

Sprinkle individual servings with chopped parsley and cheese. Makes about 12 cups.

Ratatouille

France   *Pictured on front cover*

Just pronouncing the name of this Provençal classic gets dinner off to a jovial start. But whether your French is suave or sputtering, you're sure to relish this divinely seasoned harvest celebration, served either hot or at room temperature. Crunchy Whole Wheat Baguettes (page 83) are perfect companions.

          About 2 tablespoons pine nuts
        4 tablespoons olive oil
        1 medium-size onion, chopped
        3 large cloves garlic, minced or pressed
        1 teaspoon thyme leaves
        1 small eggplant (about ¾ lb.) unpeeled, cut into ½-inch cubes
        1 large green or red bell pepper, seeded and chopped
        1 large zucchini, chopped
        2 cups chopped spinach leaves
        3 large tomatoes (about 1 lb. *total*), chopped
        ¼ cup minced parsley
          Salt and pepper
          Fresh basil
          Lemon wedges or grated lemon peel

Place pine nuts in a pan over medium heat. Cook, stirring, until lightly browned (about 5 minutes).

Heat 2 tablespoons of the oil in a wide frying pan over medium heat. Add onion and garlic, and cook, stirring, until onion is soft (about 3 minutes). Stir in remaining 2 tablespoons oil, thyme, eggplant, and green pepper, and continue cooking, stirring occasionally, for 5 more minutes. Add zucchini, spinach, tomatoes, and parsley. Reduce heat and simmer, uncovered, stirring occasionally, until vegetables are tender (about 30 minutes). Season with salt and pepper to taste.

Serve hot or at room temperature. Garnish with basil and pine nuts and pass lemon wedges at the table. Makes about 4 cups.

For a Caribbean feast, *Black Bean & Rice Soup (page 37) from Jamaica. Each bowlful will be decorated deliciously with sliced radishes and green onions, a squeeze of lime juice, and a dollop of sour cream. To accompany it all, Country Corn Muffins (page 81) from the United States.*

Grains, Pasta & Legumes

Mainstay nourishment around the globe

Centuries of human reliance on basic staples of the field have handed down a kitchenful of delicious, infinitely varied recipes using grains, legumes, and pasta. From these staples come most of the substantial and sophisticated entrées in vegetarian cooking everywhere.

Besides filling you up, as they fill the role once taken by meat, these staples can be exciting in both flavor and appearance. You can present them by themselves (with only seasonings, nuts, or seeds), topped with a sauce (you'll find recipes on pages 54 and 55), or as part of a more elaborate dish, such as Rolled Lasagne with Pesto.

Largest of the world's crops, rice and wheat turn up in cuisines from places as far apart as New Delhi and Helsinki, Iowa and Southeast Asia. But less familiar grains, often cultivated where neither rice nor wheat thrives, also appear in our recipes (and are described, with cooking directions, on page 45).

Pasta, usually made from wheat flour, is most famous as a parade of whimsically shaped noodles from Italy. We tell you how to make your own (page 52), with results so delicious that making pasta may become a habit.

Legumes—seeds packed plump with protein, vitamins, and minerals—are more commonly known in the kitchen as beans, peas, lentils, and peanuts. In addition to recipes showing off legumes' versatility, we've included a section on soaking and cooking them (page 49), since times vary considerably.

Felafil

Arab countries, Israel

In the Middle East, where garbanzo beans have provided protein since ancient times, this savory blend with bulgur wheat is a widely consumed classic. Ordinarily deep-fried, the crunchy little balls then fill up pocket bread; our version is only lightly fried, and we changed the shape to a patty.

For the Tahini Sauce, you can make your own tahini, if you wish, by whirling ½ cup toasted sesame seeds and ¼ cup olive oil in a blender or food processor until smooth.

> Tahini Sauce (recipe follows)
> Felafil Relish (recipe follows)
> ½ cup bulgur wheat
> 2 cups cooked, drained garbanzo beans (page 49) or 1 can (about 15 oz.) garbanzo beans, drained
> 3 cloves garlic, minced or pressed
> ¼ cup lemon juice
> 1 teaspoon *each* ground cumin, salt, and crushed, dried red chiles
> 2 eggs
> ½ cup fine dry bread crumbs
> 3 tablespoons finely chopped fresh coriander (cilantro)
> Salad oil
> 6 six-inch pocket breads, warmed and halved

Prepare Tahini Sauce and Felafil Relish. Place bulgur in a small bowl and add boiling water to cover. Let stand for 20 minutes. Meanwhile, in a blender or food processor combine garbanzos, garlic, lemon juice, cumin, salt, and chiles; whirl until smooth. Drain bulgur well. In a medium-size bowl, beat eggs; then mix in bread crumbs, puréed garbanzo mixture, coriander, and bulgur.

Shape mixture into six 4-inch patties. Into a wide frying pan over medium-high heat, pour oil to a depth of ¼ inch. When oil is hot, add patties and cook, turning once, until well browned (about 4 minutes on each side). Serve immediately.

To serve, cut patties in half and place each piece in a warm pocket bread half. Pass Tahini Sauce and Felafil Relish at the table. Makes 6 servings.

Tahini Sauce. Stir together 6 tablespoons **sesame tahini** and ¼ cup **water** until smooth. Mix in 1½ tablespoons **lemon juice**; 1½ teaspoons **olive oil**; 1 small clove **garlic**, minced or pressed; and a dash of **ground red pepper** (cayenne). Season to taste with **salt.** Makes about ¾ cup.

Felafil Relish. In a bowl, combine 2 medium-size **tomatoes,** peeled, seeded, and finely chopped; 1 cup finely chopped **cucumber;** and ¼ cup *each* finely chopped **green pepper, onion,** and minced **parsley.** If made ahead, cover and refrigerate for up to 3 hours. Just before serving, season to taste with **salt** and **pepper.** Serve cold or at room temperature. Makes about 3 cups.

Dalmatian Rice & Caper Salad

Yugoslavia

Located in western Yugoslavia, Dalmatia offers the world not only speckled firemen's dogs, but nippy little capers as well. The latter grow in abundance on dainty vines that decorate the crevices of ancient Dalmatian buildings.

> 6 cups cooked brown rice (page 45), cooled
> ½ cup finely chopped green onions (including tops)
> 1 cup diced, peeled cucumber
> 1 large tomato, cored and diced
> ¼ cup drained capers
> ⅓ cup olive oil
> 3 tablespoons white wine vinegar
> 2 large cloves garlic, minced or pressed
> ½ teaspoon *each* dry mustard, sugar, salt, and thyme leaves
> ¼ teaspoon ground sage
> ⅛ teaspoon pepper
> Few drops of liquid hot pepper seasoning
> Lettuce leaves (optional)
> 3 hard-cooked eggs, quartered

In a large bowl, combine rice, onions, cucumber, tomato, and capers. In a small jar with a tight-fitting lid, combine oil, vinegar, garlic, mustard, sugar, salt, thyme, sage, pepper, and hot pepper seasoning. Cover, shake well, and pour over rice mixture. Stir lightly to coat rice thoroughly.

Mound rice mixture on lettuce leaves, if desired. If made ahead, cover and let stand at room temperature for up to 3 hours. Garnish with eggs and serve at room temperature. Makes 10 to 12 servings.

Bulgur & Mint Salad

Lebanon

Known as *tabbuli,* this crunchy bulgur salad appears in different versions throughout the Middle East. Our version is the perfect warm-weather lunch or supper.

(Continued on next page)

1 cup *each* bulgur wheat and water
⅓ cup olive oil
¼ cup lemon juice
1 cup *each* finely chopped parsley and green onions (including tops)
2 large tomatoes, seeded and diced
¼ cup chopped fresh mint or 1½ tablespoons dry mint
   Salt
   Romaine lettuce
   Plain yogurt

In a small pan, combine bulgur and water; bring to a boil over high heat. Reduce heat to medium and simmer, covered, until liquid is absorbed (about 5 minutes; bulgur will still be crunchy). In a bowl, mix prepared bulgur, oil, and lemon juice; let cool.

Add parsley, onions, tomatoes, and mint; mix lightly. Season to taste with salt. Cover and refrigerate for at least 1 hour or up to 6 hours to blend flavors. For each serving, spoon some of the mixture onto romaine leaves and garnish with a dollop of yogurt. Makes 6 servings.

Vegetable-Bean Stew with Couscous

Morocco   *Pictured on facing page*

Couscous, a grain derived from semolina (coarsely milled hard wheat), is a staple in North Africa. Look for couscous in imported food sections of supermarkets; or substitute rice or bulgur wheat.

¼ cup salad oil
1 large onion, finely chopped
1 *each* large red and green bell pepper, seeded and chopped
1 teaspoon ground coriander
½ teaspoon ground cinnamon
2 medium-size sweet potatoes, peeled and cut into ½-inch cubes
2 large tomatoes, peeled and chopped
¼ cup water
1 tablespoon lemon juice
½ teaspoon saffron threads
2 cups cooked, drained garbanzo beans (page 49) or 1 can (about 15 oz.) garbanzo beans, drained
   Salt
   Hot Pepper Sauce (recipe follows)
1 medium-size zucchini, chopped
4 cups hot cooked couscous (prepared according to package directions) or hot cooked brown rice, bulgur, or millet (page 45)

Heat oil in a 5-quart kettle over medium heat; add onion, red and green bell peppers, coriander, and cinnamon and cook, stirring occasionally, until on-

ion is soft (about 5 minutes). Stir in sweet potatoes and cook, stirring often, for 2 minutes. Add tomatoes, water, lemon juice, saffron, and garbanzos. Season to taste with salt. Cover, reduce heat, and simmer for 15 more minutes.

Meanwhile, prepare Hot Pepper Sauce.

Mix zucchini into potato mixture and cook, covered, until sweet potatoes are tender (about 5 more minutes). Add more salt, if desired.

To serve, spread couscous around edge of a deep platter and spoon vegetable mixture into center. Pass Hot Pepper Sauce at the table. Makes 6 servings.

Hot Pepper Sauce. In a small pan, combine ⅓ cup **olive oil** or salad oil; 2½ teaspoons **ground red pepper** (cayenne); 1½ teaspoons ground **cumin**; 1 clove **garlic,** minced or pressed; and ¼ teaspoon **salt.** Cook over medium-low heat, stirring, until ingredients are well blended (5 minutes). Serve warm or at room temperature. Makes about ½ cup.

Kasha-stuffed Cabbage Rolls

Russia   *Pictured on page 46*

In Russia, *kasha*—steamed buckwheat groats—is often added to thin soups for substance, but here the versatile grain is used as a filling. The sour salt called for in the sauce recipe is crystallized citric acid from lemons or limes; it's available in Jewish delicatessens.

1 large head cabbage (2½ to 3 lbs.), cored
   Sweet-Sour Sauce (recipe follows)
2 tablespoons butter or margarine
1 large onion, finely chopped
½ pound mushrooms, chopped
½ teaspoon marjoram leaves
¼ teaspoon ground nutmeg
⅛ teaspoon pepper
2 cups cooked buckwheat groats (*kasha*, page 45)
1 egg, lightly beaten
   Salt
   Sour cream (optional)

(Continued on page 44)

Saffron-gilded vegetables *and a hot pepper sauce turn couscous into a Moroccan feast. As dessert, all you need are simple, sweet nibbles: dates, figs, and other fruits, with Almond Crescent Cookies (page 92). The recipe for Vegetable-Bean Stew with Couscous is on this page.*

In a 6 to 8-quart kettle, bring 4 to 5 quarts water to a boil over high heat. Add cabbage and cook, submerging with a spoon, for 15 seconds; then remove from pot. When cool enough to handle, peel off softened outer leaves (3 or 4), being careful not to tear them. Repeat with remaining cabbage until you have 12 to 14 large leaves (save remaining cabbage for other uses).

Place 4 of the leaves in the boiling water and cook until soft but still pliable (3 to 4 minutes). Drain well. Repeat with remaining leaves. Cut off and discard thick stem end of each leaf.

Prepare Sweet-Sour Sauce and set aside. Melt butter in a wide frying pan over medium heat. Add onion, mushrooms, and marjoram; cook, stirring often, until onions are soft, mushrooms are lightly browned, and liquid evaporates. Remove from heat and blend in nutmeg, pepper, groats, and egg. Season to taste with salt.

Pour about two-thirds of the Sweet-Sour Sauce into a lightly greased 9 by 13-inch baking dish. To make cabbage rolls, place about ¼ cup of the buckwheat mixture in the cupped side of the larger cabbage leaves, a little less in the smaller ones. Fold stem end over filling, then fold sides over, and roll to enclose filling. Place cabbage rolls, seam side down, in sauce. Drizzle remaining sauce evenly over rolls.

Cover tightly with foil and bake in a 350° oven for 1½ hours. Spoon some of the sauce over each serving. Pass sour cream at the table, if desired. Makes 6 servings.

Sweet-Sour Sauce. In a medium-size pan, combine 2 cans (8 oz. *each*) **tomato sauce**, 1 cup **water**, ½ cup fine **gingersnap crumbs**, ¼ cup **raisins**, 3 tablespoons firmly packed **brown sugar**, and ¾ teaspoon crushed **sour salt** (*or* substitute ¼ cup lemon juice). Bring to a boil over medium-high heat, then reduce heat and simmer, uncovered, stirring occasionally, for 5 minutes. If made ahead, let cool, cover, and refrigerate until next day.

Potato & Egg Curry

India

Aromatic with Eastern spices, this classic Indian mélange of seasoned vegetables is most authentic when made with the clarified butter (*ghee*) and spooned over India's *Basmati* rice (available in specialty food stores). From the suggested condiments, offer sweet and hot Mango Chutney for lovers of spicy foods, and crunchy Cucumber Raita to help cool the palate afterwards.

3 tablespoons clarified butter (directions follow) or salad oil

3 large, thin-skinned potatoes (about 2 lbs. *total*), peeled and diced

3 large cloves garlic, minced or pressed

1 tablespoon ground coriander

⅓ cup water

1 teaspoon *each* salt, turmeric, and ground cumin

¼ teaspoon ground red pepper (cayenne)

1½ cups water

½ cup unsweetened coconut milk

2 tablespoons lemon juice
Basmati rice (recipe follows) or cooked brown (page 45) or white rice

2 tablespoons *each* finely chopped parsley and chives

1½ cups fresh shelled peas or frozen peas, thawed

4 hard-cooked eggs, coarsely chopped
Condiments (suggestions follow)

Heat clarified butter in a 4 to 5-quart kettle over medium heat. Add potatoes and garlic, and cook, stirring, for 10 minutes. Add coriander and cook, stirring, for 1 more minute. Pour in the ⅓ cup water and cook, stirring often, until liquid evaporates. Sprinkle salt, turmeric, cumin, and cayenne over potatoes, then add the 1½ cups water, coconut milk, and lemon juice. Bring to a boil over high heat; cover, reduce heat, and boil gently until potatoes are tender (about 15 minutes).

Prepare Basmati rice.

Stir in parsley, chives, and peas. Blend in about three-fourths of the eggs and cook until heated through. Serve over rice and sprinkle with remaining eggs. Pass condiments at the table. Makes 6 servings.

Clarified butter. Melt ½ cup (¼ lb.) **butter** in a small pan over very low heat. As milky foam rises, skim it off and discard it. Pour off the clear, golden melted butter, discarding white milky solids at bottom of pan. If made ahead, cover and refrigerate; keeps for several weeks. Makes about 6 tablespoons.

Basmati rice. In a sieve, rinse 1⅓ cups **Basmati rice** with cold running water until water runs clear. In a medium-size pan, combine 2⅔ cups **water** and ½ teaspoon **salt;** bring to a boil over high heat. Stir in rice, cover, reduce heat, and simmer until liquid is absorbed and rice is tender (about 10 minutes). Stir in 1½ tablespoons **butter** or margarine. Serve immediately. Makes about 4 cups.

Condiments. Offer 3 or 4 of the following: chopped roasted **cashews** or peanuts, **raisins**, toasted **unsweetened coconut, Mango Chutney** (page 55), and **Cucumber Raita** (page 54).

Cooking Good-for-You Grains

Grains provide the world's population with an amazing 50 percent of its protein. Lacking only the essential amino acid lysine (for which you can compensate as explained on page 7), grains pack in carbohydrates, a wealth of B vitamins (but not B-12), minerals, fiber, and a trace of fat.

What counts nutritionally is to partake mainly of unrefined, whole-grain products; choose brown rice over white, for example.

A few hints about cooking grains. *Yield:* 1 uncooked grain will yield about 3 cups cooked grain.

Salt: To cooking water, add about ¼ teaspoon salt for each cup of uncooked grain. *Cooking option:* One alternative to simple boiling is to cook grains (bulgur, buckwheat, millet, and of course, rice) like a pilaf. Sauté dry grains first in butter, margarine, or salad oil (about 1 tablespoon per cup); then, instead of water, add boiling Root Vegetable Stock or instant vegetable stock (page 33), cover, and simmer until grain is tender to bite. *Doneness:* Taste all grains after the minimum cooking time; if you prefer a softer texture, continue cooking, tasting often, until done to your liking.

Name	Description	How to Cook
Barley	Pearl variety: mild, starchy flavor. Hulled variety: nutty flavor. Use both in soups, stews, casseroles.	2 parts water to 1 part barley. Bring to a boil, cover, reduce heat, simmer 40 to 45 minutes; let stand, covered, 5 to 10 minutes.
Brown Rice	Unpolished; long and short grain; sweet, nutty flavor. Use in soups, stews, casseroles, or baked goods, or with sauces.	2 parts water to 1 part brown rice. Bring to a boil, cover, reduce heat, simmer 35 to 40 minutes; let stand, covered, 5 to 10 minutes. Or see "Cooking option," above.
Buckwheat (kasha)	Not a true grain but a member of a herbaceous plant family; available untoasted or toasted; strong, distinct flavor. Use in casseroles or with sauces.	Cook as directed for bulgur, but only 10 to 12 minutes. Or, in an ungreased frying pan, mix 2 cups buckwheat and 1 beaten egg; cook, stirring, over high heat, 2 minutes; add boiling stock or water; cover, reduce heat, cook 12 to 15 minutes.
Bulgur (bulgur wheat)	Wheat berries that have been steamed, dried, and cracked; delicate, nutty flavor. Use in casseroles, baked goods, or salads.	1½ parts water to 1 part bulgur. Bring to a boil, cover, reduce heat, simmer 12 to 15 minutes. Or see "Cooking option," above.
Cracked Wheat	Similar to bulgur, but not steamed before being cracked. Use as bulgur.	Same as directed for bulgur.
Millet	Mild, delicate flavor. Use in stuffings, casseroles, or baked goods, or with sauces.	2½ parts water to 1 part millet. Bring to a boil, cover, reduce heat, simmer 18 to 20 minutes. Or see "Cooking option," above.
Oats	Rolled, quick-cooking, or groats (steel cut); mild flavor, creamy. Use as cereal or in baked goods.	1 part boiling water to 1 part rolled or quick-cooking oats (or use up to 2 parts boiling water for creamier consistency); cover, reduce heat, simmer 3 to 10 minutes. Soak 1 part groats in 2 parts water for 1 hour; bring to a boil, cover, reduce heat, simmer 25 to 30 minutes.
Rye and Triticale	Both have strong, tangy flavor; triticale (hybrid wheat and rye containing more protein than either parent grain) is slightly milder. Use in casseroles and baked goods.	3 parts water to 1 part rye or triticale; bring to a boil, cover, reduce heat, simmer 1 to 1¼ hours. If too dry, add water, continue cooking. If too moist, drain well.
Whole Wheat (wheat berries)	Nutty, mild flavor; chewy texture. Use in casseroles, stews, or baked goods, or with sauces.	3 parts water to 1 part whole wheat; bring to a boil, cover, reduce heat, simmer 2 hours. If too dry, add water, continue cooking. If too moist, drain well.

Stroganoff with Spinach

...w dishes would be complete ...ddition of mushrooms. And ...cking stroganoff, the mush-...bright-colored beet or carrot ...longside, and our favorite ...is Basque Sheepherder's

...margarine
...nced or pressed

...g
...ly sliced
...k or instant vegetable

...Swiss chard leaves,

...asoning

...& Soy Pasta
...ked brown rice

Remo... ...; cut in half
length... ...rthwise so
that it...

Melt... ...over me-
dium he... ...ok, stir-
ring often... ...x in pa-
prika and... ...nion is
soft but no... ...cook,
stirring occ... ...s and
mushrooms... ...tes).

Add stock... ...eat.
Reduce heat... ...ing
gently until liq... ...to
8 more minutes... ...til
wilted. Blend in... d
hot pepper seas...
Cook, stirring, ju...
boil. Serve over p...

Alongside the samovar is traditional peasant fare that's fit for royalty. In the tureen are Kasha-stuffed Cabbage Rolls (page 42) from Russia. From neighboring Finland come savory Carrot-filled Rye Pastries to spread with Finnish Egg Butter (page 18).

Colorful Fried Rice

China

Long before the current vogue for Chinese cuisine, most people in the United States were familiar with at least a few favorites: won ton soup, chow mein, and—to many, most savory of all—fried rice. Garnished with sesame seeds, well laced with stir-fried vegetables, and made with brown rice, the dish is sure to become a favorite.

   3 **tablespoons sesame seeds**
      About 3 tablespoons salad oil
   1 **cup thinly sliced carrots**
   1 **medium-size onion, thinly sliced and separated into rings**
   2 **cloves garlic, minced or pressed**
   1 **large green pepper, seeded and cut into thin strips**
   1 **cup *each* thinly sliced zucchini and thinly sliced mushrooms**
   2 **cups bean sprouts**
   1 **cup hot cooked brown rice (page 45)**
   1 **teaspoon grated fresh ginger**
  ¼ **cup soy sauce**
   3 **tablespoons fresh coriander (cilantro)**

Spread the sesame seeds in a small frying pan over medium heat. Cook, shaking pan often, until seeds are golden (about 2 minutes); set aside.

Prepare remaining ingredients before you begin cooking.

Heat 1 tablespoon of the oil in a wok or wide frying pan over high heat. Add carrots and stir-fry (cook, stirring constantly) for 1 minute. Mix in onion, garlic, and green pepper and stir-fry for 1 more minute, adding more oil as needed. Add zucchini and mushrooms and stir-fry until all vegetables are just tender-crisp (about 2 more minutes). Mix in bean sprouts and rice and cook, stirring, until heated through.

In a small bowl, mix ginger with soy; blend into rice mixture. Serve immediately, sprinkled with coriander and sesame seeds. Makes 4 to 6 servings.

White Bean Salad

France   *Pictured on page 74*

A garlicky, herb-flecked marinade imparts its tangy flavor to these beans. For an elegant spring or summer lunch, serve the salad with bread, deviled eggs, and a selection of cheeses.

(Continued on next page)

½ cup olive oil

3 tablespoons red wine vinegar

2 tablespoons chopped chives

3 cloves garlic, minced or pressed

1 teaspoon dry tarragon

⅛ teaspoon freshly grated nutmeg or ground nutmeg

½ teaspoon *each* salt and honey

Dash of liquid hot pepper seasoning

5 cups cooked small white beans (page 49), cooled

⅓ cup finely chopped parsley

Lettuce leaves

In a jar with a tight-fitting lid, combine oil, vinegar, chives, garlic, tarragon, nutmeg, salt, honey and hot pepper seasoning. Cover and shake well.

Place beans in a large bowl. Mix in dressing and parsley. Let stand at room temperature until flavors are blended (about 1 hour). If made ahead, cover and refrigerate for up to 6 hours; bring to room temperature before serving.

To serve, mound salad on lettuce leaves. Makes 4 to 6 servings.

Lentil Salad

Egypt

A staple protein source in North Africa and the Middle East, lentils are served there in every conceivable fashion—here, for example, in a zesty salad.

2 cups (12-oz. package) lentils

6 cups water

2 whole cloves garlic, peeled

2 bay leaves

1 cup thinly sliced green onions (including tops)

1 small fresh hot green chile, seeded and finely chopped

½ cup olive oil

2 tablespoons red wine vinegar

1 teaspoon grated lime peel

2 tablespoons lime juice

3 large cloves garlic, minced or pressed

1 teaspoon ground cumin

Salt

2 tablespoons finely chopped parsley

Rinse lentils; sort through and discard any foreign material. Drain well. In a 4-quart pan, combine lentils, water, the 2 cloves garlic, and bay leaves. Bring to a boil over high heat. Cover, reduce heat, and simmer until lentils are tender (25 to 30 minutes). Drain well, then discard garlic and bay leaves. Let lentils cool for 15 to 20 minutes.

Transfer to a large bowl and mix lightly with onions and chile. In a jar with a tight-fitting lid, combine oil, vinegar, lime peel and juice, the minced garlic, and cumin. Cover, shake well, and pour over lentils. Stir mixture lightly. Season to taste with salt. Cover and let stand at room temperature until flavors are blended (about 1 hour). If made ahead, cover and refrigerate until next day; bring to room temperature before serving. Just before serving, garnish with parsley. Makes 4 to 6 entrée servings or 8 side-dish servings.

Greens & Tofu in Peanut Sauce

Thailand

In this regional specialty, an intriguing blend of peanuts and coconut invites your delicious discovery. Buy crisp onion flakes in an Oriental grocery, or use ½ cup Crisp-fried Onions (page 15).

⅓ cup crunchy peanut butter

1 small can (7 ¾ oz.) sweetened coconut milk

2 cloves garlic, minced or pressed

1½ tablespoons *each* white vinegar and soy sauce

1 teaspoon grated fresh ginger or ¼ teaspoon ground ginger

⅛ to ¼ teaspoon ground red pepper (cayenne)

1 tablespoon peanut oil or salad oil

2 cups *each* thinly shredded cabbage and spinach

½ cup thinly sliced green onions (including tops)

2 cups bean sprouts

½ pound firm tofu, cut into ½-inch cubes

8 ounces rice vermicelli or Chinese wheat flour noodles, cooked, or 4 to 5 cups hot cooked rice (page 45)

½ cup crisp onion flakes (optional)

In a small pan, combine peanut butter, coconut milk, garlic, vinegar, and soy. Cook, stirring, over medium heat until well combined, then continue cooking, uncovered, for 3 minutes. Remove from heat and add ginger and red pepper.

Heat oil in a wide frying pan over medium heat. Add cabbage and spinach and cook, stirring often, until greens are slightly wilted (about 2 minutes). Stir in onions and bean sprouts, then add tofu and peanut sauce; stir gently to mix well. Cover and cook just until heated through.

Serve over noodles and, if desired, sprinkle with onion flakes. Makes 4 to 6 servings.

Note: To cook rice vermicelli, bring 3 quarts water to a boil over high heat. Add noodles and cook, stirring occasionally, until tender (3 to 5 minutes). Drain and rinse with hot water, drain again, and serve immediately.

How Long to Simmer Legumes

At very low cost, legumes pack in a powerhouse of protein—a navy bean, for example, is 20 percent protein. One legume—the soybean—is said to be a perfect source of protein, and legumes in general have almost perfect protein, lacking only methionine, an essential amino acid easily furnished by a side serving of cheese, milk, or whole grain bread.

Legumes also offer plenty of iron, calcium, potassium, and B vitamins in a caloric package equivalent to that of potatoes. High in fiber, they're low in sodium and entirely innocent of cholesterol.

Ideal a food as they may sound, legumes do come with a couple of small inconveniences. Some people find them hard to digest at first, though adequate presoaking and cooking help. This long soaking-cooking time is the other drawback, but you can always opt for the quicker method listed below. And lentils and split peas, speediest to prepare, require no soaking at all.

Rinse, sort through, and discard any imperfect legumes before soaking. Cooking times given on packages will vary and may differ from those we list for individual types. Simply test for doneness after the minimum suggested time; legumes should be tender to bite.

Soaking legumes

Quick soaking. For each pound **dry legumes,** bring 8 cups **water** to a boil. Add washed and sorted legumes and boil for 2 minutes. Remove from heat, cover pan, and let stand for 1 hour. Drain and rinse legumes, discarding water.

Overnight soaking. For each pound **dry legumes,** dissolve 2 teaspoons **salt** in 6 cups **water.** Add washed and sorted legumes; soak until next day. Drain and rinse legumes, discarding water.

Cooking legumes

For each pound dry legumes (weight before soaking), dissolve 2 teaspoons **salt** in 6 cups **water;** bring to a boil. Add **soaked legumes** and boil gently, with pan lid partially on, until tender (individual cooking times follow). Add more water if needed to keep beans submerged. If desired, season to taste with salt after legumes have cooked. Drain. Makes 6 to 7 cups cooked legumes.

Black beans. Popular in Caribbean, Central, and South American cooking. Robust flavor. Soak. Cook for 1 to 1½ hours.

Black-eyed peas. Smooth texture, pealike flavor, good mixed with other vegetables. Soak. Cook for about 1 hour.

Garbanzo beans (chickpeas, ceci beans). Popular in Middle East, Africa. Firm texture, nutlike flavor. Good in minestrone, salads. Soak. Cook for 2 to 2½ hours.

Great Northern (white) beans. Mild flavor, good in soups, combined with other vegetables. Soak. Cook for 1 to 1½ hours.

Kidney beans. Firm texture, hearty flavor. Hold shape well in chili dishes, casseroles. Soak. Cook for 1 to 1½ hours.

Lentils. Popular in Middle East, India, Europe. Mild flavor blends well with many foods, spices. No soaking needed. Cook for 25 to 30 minutes.

Limas, baby. Use like other white beans in soups, casseroles. Soak. Cook for ¾ to 1¼ hours.

Pink, pinto, and red beans. Popular in Mexican cooking. Hearty flavor, good in barbecue-style beans, soups, casseroles. Soak. Cook for 1¼ to 1½ hours.

Soybeans. Ancient crop of Asia. Strong-flavored. Soak in refrigerator overnight. Cook for 3 to 3½ hours.

Split peas, green and yellow. Good for soups, side dishes. No soaking needed. Cook for 35 to 45 minutes.

White beans (navy), small. Hold shape well; classic for baked beans. Soak. Cook for about 1 hour.

Lentil & Bulgur Pilaf

Lebanon

People from many parts of the world traditionally serve grains with legumes to create what nutritionists call "complementary protein." Here, in a hearty pilaf, is one example from the Middle East.

- ½ cup lentils
  Salt
- 3 tablespoons butter or margarine
- 1 medium-size onion, finely chopped
- 1 red or green bell pepper, seeded and chopped
- ½ teaspoon *each* ground allspice and ground cumin
- 2 cloves garlic, minced or pressed
- 1 cup bulgur wheat
- ½ teaspoon salt
- 1 teaspoon grated lemon peel
- 2 tablespoons sesame tahini (see Felafil, page 41)
- 1½ cups boiling water
- 2 tablespoons lemon juice
- 6 eggs
  Minced parsley

In a small pan, combine lentils and 2 cups water. Bring to a boil over high heat; then reduce heat, cover, and continue boiling gently until tender (25 to 30 minutes). Drain; season to taste with salt.

Melt butter in a wide frying pan (with a cover) over low heat. Add onion, bell pepper, allspice, and cumin and cook, stirring, until onion is soft and lightly browned. Add garlic, bulgur, and the ½ teaspoon salt; cook, stirring to coat bulgur with onion mixture, for 1 to 2 more minutes.

In a medium-size bowl, stir together lemon peel, tahini, and boiling water; add to bulgur mixture and stir until well combined. Cover tightly and cook over low heat until liquid is absorbed and bulgur is tender (about 5 minutes). Stir in lentils and lemon juice and cook until mixture is heated through.

Just before serving, poach eggs. Spoon pilaf onto a warm platter, and in it make 6 indentations. Place drained eggs in them, and sprinkle parsley over all. Makes 6 servings.

Stir-fried Tofu & Vegetables

Vietnam

A stir-fried combination of tofu and colorful, tender-crisp vegetables costs only a pittance. This is but one variation of *rau xao,* and it's made with vegetables available in North American markets.

- ½ pound medium-firm tofu, cut into ½-inch cubes
- 3 tablespoons soy sauce
- 1 teaspoon rice vinegar or white vinegar
- ¼ teaspoon ground cumin
- 2 cloves garlic, minced or pressed
- ½ teaspoon grated fresh ginger or ⅛ teaspoon ground ginger
- 3 tablespoons peanut oil or salad oil
- 1 large carrot, chopped
- 2 cups thinly sliced broccoli stems and bite-size flowerets
- 1 cup *each* bean sprouts and sliced mushrooms
- ½ cup thinly sliced green onions (including tops)
- 3 tablespoons minced fresh coriander (cilantro)

Place tofu in a shallow bowl. In another bowl, mix soy, vinegar, cumin, garlic, and ginger; drizzle over tofu. Set aside while you prepare remaining ingredients for cooking.

Heat oil in a wok or wide frying pan over high heat. Add carrot and stir-fry (cook, stirring constantly) for 1 minute; add broccoli and continue stir-frying for 2 more minutes. Then mix in bean sprouts, mushrooms, and green onions. Stir-fry for 30 more seconds, then reduce heat to medium-high. Add tofu mixture and cook, stirring gently, just until tofu is heated through but vegetables are still crisp (1 to 2 minutes). Garnish with coriander. Makes 4 servings.

Pasta with Nut Sauce

Mexico

In Mexican cuisine, nuts sometimes serve as a thickener for sauce. Here, they add their rich flavors to garlic in a nutritious sauce that mixes and coats perfectly when it's spooned over pasta.

- ½ cup *each* walnuts and blanched almonds
- ⅓ cup pine nuts
- 1 cup whipping cream
- 2 cloves garlic, minced or pressed
- ¼ teaspoon salt
- ⅛ teaspoon white pepper
  1 recipe Basic Egg Pasta (page 52), cut into fettuccine-width noodles, or 8 ounces packaged fettuccine
  Grated Parmesan cheese
  Lime wedges

Spread walnuts, almonds, and pine nuts in a shallow pan and toast in a 350° oven for 8 to 10 minutes or until lightly browned. Let cool slightly.

In a blender or food processor, combine nuts, cream, garlic, salt, and pepper. Whirl until smooth. If made ahead, cover and refrigerate until next day; bring to room temperature before using.

Cook pasta according to directions on page 52 or on package; drain well and immediately mix lightly with sauce to coat pasta. Pass Parmesan cheese and lime wedges at the table. Makes 4 to 6 servings.

Vegetable-topped Crisp Noodles

China

This dish looks like Asia's answer to pizza: oven-crisped noodles create a crust, which you top with stir-fried vegetables and tofu. You can use any thin Oriental noodle, such as Japanese *chuka soba*.

> Cooking Sauce (recipe follows)
> 1¼ pounds broccoli
> 10 to 12 ounces thin Oriental noodles
> 2 tablespoons sesame oil or salad oil
> ½ teaspoon salt
> 5 tablespoons salad oil
> 1 clove garlic, minced or pressed
> 1 medium-size onion, chopped
> 2 stalks celery, cut diagonally into ¼-inch-thick slices
> 2 medium-size carrots, cut diagonally into ¼-inch-thick slices
> 1 red or green bell pepper, seeded and cut into ¼-inch-wide strips
> 3 tablespoons water
> ¼ pound mushrooms, sliced
> 1 pound medium-firm tofu, well drained and cut into ¾-inch cubes

Prepare ingredients, including Cooking Sauce, before you begin cooking.

Cut off broccoli flowerets; peel off and discard tough outside layer of stalks, then cut stalks into ¼-inch-thick slices. Slice large broccoli flowerets in half or thirds lengthwise.

Cook noodles according to package directions; drain well. In a large bowl, toss noodles with sesame oil and salt.

About 30 minutes before serving, place a 14-inch pizza pan or a 10 by 15-inch rimmed baking sheet in oven while it preheats to 500°. When pan is very hot, pour in 2 tablespoons of the salad oil; tilt pan to coat bottom and sides. Spread cooked noodles in an even round in pan and bake, uncovered, on bottom rack for 25 to 30 minutes or until golden on top and bottom.

About 8 to 10 minutes before noodles are done, heat 2 more tablespoons of the salad oil in a wok or wide frying pan (at least 12 inches in diameter) over high heat. Add garlic, onion, celery, carrots, bell pepper, and broccoli stems. Stir-fry (cook, stirring constantly) for 2 minutes. Add water, cover, and cook, stirring often, for about 3 more minutes.

Add the remaining 1 tablespoon salad oil, broccoli flowerets, and mushrooms. Stir-fry for 1 more minute. Stir Cooking Sauce and add to vegetable mixture. Add tofu and cook, stirring gently, until sauce boils and thickens.

To serve, run a long spatula under noodle pancake to loosen it, then slide it onto a cutting board and, with a sharp knife, cut it into 6 equal wedges. Arrange pancake pieces on a serving plate and top with vegetable mixture. Makes 6 servings.

Cooking Sauce. In a bowl, combine 3 tablespoons **cornstarch;** 1 clove **garlic,** minced or pressed; 1½ teaspoons **ground ginger;** 2 tablespoons **soy sauce;** ⅛ teaspoon **ground red pepper** (cayenne); ¼ cup **dry sherry;** and 2½ cups **Root Vegetable Stock** or instant vegetable stock (page 33).

Rolled Lasagne with Pesto

Italy

Lasagne with its noodles filled, rolled into individual servings, and baked is still lasagne. And still delicious, as you'll find out when you try this recipe with pesto, the famed garlicky basil-Parmesan sauce.

> 12 lasagne noodles (Basic Egg Pasta, page 52, or packaged)
> 1 egg
> 2 cups (1 lb.) ricotta cheese
> 2 cups (8 oz.) shredded jack cheese
> ¾ teaspoon oregano leaves
> 3 tablespoons minced parsley
> 2 cloves garlic, minced or pressed
> ⅔ cup *each* whipping cream and Pesto (page 55)

Cook noodles according to directions on page 52 or on package. Drain and set aside. When cool enough to handle, carefully separate noodles.

In a medium-size bowl, beat egg, then blend in ricotta and jack cheese, oregano, parsley, and garlic. Spread ricotta mixture evenly over each noodle. Roll from end to end. Stand rolled noodles on end in a greased shallow 8 by 10-inch baking dish.

Blend cream and Pesto; pour evenly over lasagne rolls. Cover tightly with foil and bake in a 350° oven for 30 to 35 minutes or until sauce is bubbly and rolls are heated through. Makes 6 servings.

Homemade Pasta

Pasta—ever popular—never fails to please, especially when it's homemade. Our first basic recipe takes to just about any sauce. Try Norwegian Mushroom Sauce (page 55) with Whole Wheat & Soy Pasta, and enhance Cornmeal-Parmesan Pasta with Pesto (page 55).

Basic Egg Pasta

You can make pasta dough using the traditional handmixing method, or more quickly in a food processor.

Mixing by hand. Mound 2 cups **unbleached all-purpose flour** on a work surface or in a large bowl; made a deep well in center. Break 2 large **eggs** into well. Keeping motion contained in well, beat eggs lightly with a fork; stir in 1 tablespoon **salad oil,** then 1 tablespoon **water.** Using a circular motion, begin to draw flour from sides of well. Continue mixing until all of the flour is moistened (if needed, add more water, a few drops at a time). When mixture becomes too stiff to stir, use hands to finish mixing. Pat dough into a ball. Clean work surface and flour it lightly. Knead dough until smooth and elastic (3 to 4 minutes), adding flour as needed to prevent sticking (if dough will be hand-rolled, knead for 10 minutes). Cover and let stand for 20 minutes. Divide into 4 equal portions.

Mixing in a food processor. Using metal blade, process 2 cups of **unbleached all-purpose flour,** 2 large **eggs,** and 1 tablespoon **salad oil** until mixture looks like cornmeal (about 5 seconds). With motor running, add 1 to 2 tablespoons **water,** a little at a time, through feed tube until dough forms a ball. Dough should be well blended but not sticky. If sticky, add a little flour; if crumbly, add another teaspoon or 2 of water. Turn dough out onto a floured board and knead until smooth and elastic. Cover and let stand for 20 minutes. Divide into 4 equal portions.

Rolling and cutting pasta. (To use a pasta machine, follow appliance manual directions or consult *Sunset's Pasta Cook Book* or *Italian Cook Book.*) With a rolling pin, roll out one portion of the dough into a rectangle about 1/16 inch thick. If dough is sticky, turn and flour both sides as you roll. Transfer rolled strip to a lightly floured surface or cloth; leave uncovered as you roll out remaining portions. Let each strip dry for 5 to 10 minutes until it feels leathery.

To cut, place a strip of rolled dough on a lightly floured cutting board and sprinkle with flour. Roll up jelly roll style, starting at one narrow end. Cut roll crosswise into noodle widths (about 1/4 inch for fettuccine, about 1/8 inch for tagliarini, and about 2 inches for lasagne).

Cooking homemade pasta. In a large kettle, bring 3 quarts **water** and 1 tablespoon **salt** to a boil over high heat. Add pasta slowly to boiling water; stir briefly if noodles need separating. Continue boiling, uncovered, until tender but still firm to bite (*al dente*); test by tasting 1 strand. Cooking time depends on thickness of noodles and type of flour used, but ranges from 1 to 4 minutes. (Whole Wheat & Soy lasagne noodles require 5 to 6 minutes.) If pasta is to be used hot, drain well and serve immediately. To cool pasta for a salad or lasagne, drain well, rinse with cold water, and drain again. Makes about 4 cups cooked pasta (4 to 6 servings).

Whole Wheat & Soy Pasta. This dough is difficult to roll and cut without a pasta machine.

Prepare **Basic Egg Pasta,** but omit all-purpose flour, and substitute a mixture of 1½ cups **whole wheat flour** (not stone-ground), ½ cup **soy flour,** and ¼ teaspoon **salt.** Increase **water** to 2 to 3 tablespoons.

Cornmeal-Parmesan Pasta. This dough is difficult to roll and cut without a pasta machine.

Prepare **Basic Egg Pasta,** but omit all-purpose flour, and substitute a mixture of 1½ cups **unbleached all-purpose flour,** ¼ cup **yellow cornmeal** (not stone-ground), and ¼ cup grated **Parmesan cheese.** Increase **salad oil** to 2 tablespoons and **water** to 2 to 4 tablespoons.

Spinach Lasagne

Italy

One of Italy's most copied culinary triumphs gains extra vitality in our rendition, made with whole grain pasta and spinach. A sure hit, it makes a hearty and economical company entrée to serve with Whole Wheat Baguettes (page 83), steamed green beans or broccoli spears, and a salad.

- 2 pounds spinach (about 2 large bunches)
- 2 tablespoons olive oil or salad oil
- 1 large onion, finely chopped
- 3 cloves garlic, minced or pressed
- 1 teaspoon *each* oregano leaves and dry basil
- 1 can (1 lb.) tomatoes
- ¼ cup tomato paste
- ½ cup dry red wine
- 12 lasagne noodles (Whole Wheat & Soy or Cornmeal-Parmesan, page 52, or packaged)
  Salt and freshly ground pepper
- 1 egg
- 2 cups (1 lb.) ricotta cheese
- ¼ teaspoon ground nutmeg
- 2 cups (8 oz.) shredded mozzarella or jack cheese
- 1 cup (3 oz.) grated Parmesan cheese

Remove and discard tough spinach stems. Place spinach, with water that clings to leaves, in a large deep pan. Cook over medium heat, stirring often, until wilted (2 to 4 minutes). Drain well and let cool. Chop spinach coarsely, squeezing out excess moisture. Set aside.

Heat oil in a wide frying pan over medium heat. Add onion, garlic, oregano, and basil; cook, stirring often, until onion is soft. Mix in tomatoes (break up with a spoon) and their liquid, tomato paste, and wine. Bring to a boil over high heat, then cover, reduce heat, and simmer for 20 minutes. Return to a boil and continue boiling gently, uncovered, until sauce thickens and is reduced to about 2½ cups.

Meanwhile, cook noodles according to directions on page 52 or on package. Drain and set aside. When cool enough to handle, carefully separate noodles.

Season sauce to taste with salt and pepper, then spoon about a fourth of it into a lightly greased 9 by 13-inch baking dish. Place 4 of the noodles side by side lengthwise in sauce and spread half of the spinach over them. In a small bowl, beat egg, then blend in ricotta cheese and nutmeg. Spread half of the ricotta mixture over spinach. Sprinkle with a third of the mozzarella cheese and ¼ cup of the Parmesan cheese.

Add another fourth of the tomato sauce. Top with 4 more noodles, remaining spinach, remaining ricotta mixture, another third of the mozzarella cheese, and ¼ cup more of the Parmesan cheese. Then layer, in order, remaining noodles, tomato sauce, and mozzarella and Parmesan cheese. If made ahead, cover and refrigerate until next day.

Bake, uncovered, in a 350° oven for 25 to 35 minutes (35 to 45 minutes, if refrigerated) or until hot, bubbly, and lightly browned. Cut into squares to serve. Makes 6 to 8 servings.

Rigatoni with Eggplant & Olive Sauce

Italy

The Italians are endlessly creative when it comes to sauces for their pasta. To the delight of vegetarians the world over, many of the creations are meatless, such as this glorious tomato-based eggplant sauce.

- ½ cup olive oil or salad oil
- 1 large unpeeled eggplant (about 1½ lbs.), cut into ¾-inch cubes
- 3 medium-size onions, coarsely chopped
- 3 cloves garlic, minced or pressed
- 1 large green pepper, seeded and cut into strips
- 2 cans (1 lb. *each*) Italian-style tomatoes
- 2 teaspoons sugar
- 1 tablespoon dry basil
- ½ cup finely chopped parsley
- 1 small can (2¼ oz.) sliced ripe olives, drained
- 1 can (2¼ oz.) sliced pimentos, drained
- 1 pound rigatoni or large shell macaroni
  Salt and pepper
- 1 cup (3 oz.) grated Parmesan cheese

Heat oil in a Dutch oven over medium heat; add eggplant and onions. Cook, covered, stirring often, until eggplant is very soft and lightly browned (about 25 minutes). Add garlic and green pepper and cook, stirring, for 2 more minutes.

Stir in tomatoes (break up with a spoon) and their liquid, sugar, and basil. Cover and simmer, stirring occasionally, for 15 minutes. Add parsley, olives, and pimentos; simmer, uncovered, stirring often, until sauce thickens (about 20 more minutes).

Meanwhile cook rigatoni according to package directions; drain well and turn onto a deep platter. Season eggplant mixture to taste with salt and pepper, then spoon over rigatoni; sprinkle with ¼ cup of the cheese. Serve immediately. Pass remaining cheese to sprinkle over individual servings. Makes 6 servings.

Sauces & Condiments—the Finishing Touch

Mother Nature's marvelous foods, though full of nourishment, sometimes need a boost when it comes to flavor. Be it lentils or broccoli, cracked wheat or poached eggs, their natural flavor may be too plain on its own. But a splash of zesty sauce can make all the difference between dull and terrific.

Sauce making needn't be difficult or time-consuming. Most of the sauces here are ready in minutes, and many can be made days or weeks ahead.

Here's a versatile assortment of recipes to spark both your creativity and your palate. Collected from all over the world, they range from cool and gentle to hot and spicy. Besides enhancing plain grains, beans, or pasta, many of the sauces will do wonders for steamed vegetables, omelets, or any other part of your meal that needs dressing up.

Cool Green Mayonnaise makes an exquisite salad dressing or a marvelous French accent for halved hard-cooked eggs or for vegetables. Use Mexican Cream (Mexico's answer to the French *crème fraiche*) as a substitute for sour cream, to jazz up fruit or to top entrées like enchiladas. Yogurty Cucumber Raita from India can serve as a salad on its own, or it can tone down a spicy dish, especially a curry.

Eggs come to mind immediately as a reason for making hollandaise, but on second thought, you'll come up with asparagus, broccoli, bulgur, and other partners as well. Guacamole, a Mexican favorite, adds snappy avocado appeal to any tortilla-wrapped entrée—or to a salad. Pesto (called *pistou* in France) is a basil-green and garlicky classic of northern Italy, usually spooned over pasta. Try it with sautéed summer squash or bell peppers, for a change of pace. Use our Mushroom Sauce from Norway as you might a gravy—spoon it over pilaf, pasta, vegetables, or omelets.

Match up Pimento & Parsley Sauce with omelets, vegetables, pasta, grains, and legumes. Mango Chutney, traditionally served alongside Indian curries, is equally good with plain steamed rice or couscous.

Green Mayonnaise

In a blender or food processor, combine 1 **egg,** 2 tablespoons **white wine vinegar,** ½ cup *each* lightly packed **watercress** and **parsley,** 1 sliced **green onion** (including top), ½ teaspoon *each* **dry tarragon** and **salt,** and ¾ teaspoon **Dijon mustard;** whirl until smooth.

With motor on high, add 1 cup **salad oil,** a few drops at a time at first, increasing to a slow, steady stream about ¹⁄₁₆ inch wide as mixture begins to thicken. If made ahead, cover and refrigerate for up to 1 week. Makes about 1½ cups.

Mexican Cream

Warm ½ pint (1 cup) **whipping cream** to between 90° and 100°; add 1 tablespoon **buttermilk** or sour cream, mixing well. Cover and let stand at room temperature (68° to 72°—or put in a yogurt maker) for 12 to 16 hours or until mixture starts to thicken.

Refrigerate for at least 24 hours before using to allow acid flavor to develop and cream to thicken further; cream should be of almost spreadable consistency. Store in refrigerator for up to 2 weeks or as long as taste is tangy but fresh. Makes 1 cup.

Cucumber Raita

In a small bowl, combine 1½ cups **plain yogurt,** 1 cup seeded, finely chopped **cucumber** (unpeeled unless skin is tough or waxed), 2 tablespoons thinly sliced **green onion** (including top), 1 tablespoon minced **fresh coriander** (cilantro), ¼ teaspoon **salt,** and a dash of **ground red pepper** (cayenne). Mix until ingredients are well combined. Cover and refrigerate for at least 2 hours or until next day to blend flavors. Makes about 2 cups.

Hollandaise Sauce

In a blender or food processor, combine 2 **egg yolks,** ½ teaspoon **dry mustard,** a dash of **ground red pepper** (cayenne), and 2 tablespoons **lemon juice.** Whirl at high speed until well blended. With motor on high, add ½ cup (¼ lb.) hot melted **butter,** a few drops at a time at first, increasing to a slow, steady stream about ¹⁄₁₆ inch wide as mixture begins to thicken. Serve immediately. Or if made ahead, transfer to a bowl and let stand at room temperature for up to 2 hours. To reheat, place bowl in water that's hot to touch; stir with a wire whip until sauce is slightly warmed. Serve immediately. Makes ⅔ cup.

Guacamole

In a bowl, mix 3 tablespoons **lemon or lime juice** and ⅓ cup **minced onion;** let stand for 1 hour. Peel and dice (or finely chop) 3 ripe **avocados;** add to onion mixture along with 1 large clove **garlic,** minced or pressed; 1 medium-size **tomato** (optional), peeled and diced; and 2 tablespoons minced **fresh coriander** (cilantro). If desired, mix in 1 **small fresh hot green chile,** seeded and finely chopped, or a dash of liquid hot pepper seasoning. Season to taste with **salt.** If made ahead, place a piece of plastic wrap directly on mixture and refrigerate for up to 8 hours. Serve cold or at room temperature. Makes about 2 cups.

Pesto

In a blender or food processor, place 2 cups lightly packed **fresh basil leaves,** washed and patted dry; 1 cup (3 oz.) grated **Parmesan cheese;** ½ cup **olive oil;** and 1 or 2 cloves **garlic,** minced or pressed. Whirl until basil is finely chopped and mixture is well blended. Spoon over hot cooked food. If made ahead, place in small jars and pour on a thin layer of **olive oil** to prevent darkening. Refrigerate for up to 1 week; freeze for longer storage. Makes 1⅓ cups.

Norwegian Mushroom Sauce

In a wide frying pan over medium heat, melt 3 tablespoons **butter** or margarine. Add 1 pound **mushrooms,** thinly sliced; cook, stirring often, until mushrooms are lightly browned and liquid evaporates (8 to 10 minutes). Sprinkle with 2 tablespoons **unbleached all-purpose flour,** then stir to coat mushrooms. Stirring, slowly pour in ⅔ cup **Root Vegetable Stock** or instant vegetable stock (page 33); continue stirring until stock is thickened and smooth. Remove from heat and blend in ½ cup **sour cream** or half-and-half (light cream); cook, stirring, over low heat just until heated through. Blend in 2 tablespoons **dry sherry** or dry white wine; season to taste with **salt, white pepper,** and **ground nutmeg.** Serve immediately. Makes about 2½ cups.

Venezuelan Pimento & Parsley Sauce

Heat ¼ cup **olive oil** or salad oil in a medium-size frying pan over medium heat. Add 1 large **onion,** finely chopped, and cook, stirring often, until soft. Mix in 2 cloves **garlic,** minced or pressed; 1 jar or can (4 oz.) **pimentos,** drained and chopped; ½ cup chopped **parsley;** ⅓ cup **white wine vinegar;** ½ teaspoon **salt;** and ⅛ teaspoon **pepper.** Cook, stirring, just until ingredients are heated through. Serve hot or at room temperature. If made ahead, let cool, cover, and refrigerate for up to 2 days. Makes 1¼ cups.

Mango Chutney

In a 4 to 5-quart kettle, combine 8 cups chopped fresh **mangoes** or peaches (4 to 5 large); 2 cups **apple cider vinegar;** 1 cup **raisins;** 1 small **onion,** finely chopped; 3 large cloves **garlic,** minced or pressed; and ½ cup firmly packed **brown sugar.** Bring to a boil over medium-high heat, stirring often. Reduce heat to low; cover and simmer, stirring occasionally, until mangoes are tender (about 20 minutes).

Blend in 1 teaspoon **grated fresh ginger** or ¼ teaspoon ground ginger and 1 or 2 small, dried whole hot **red chiles,** coarsely chopped. Continue simmering, uncovered, stirring occasionally as mixture thickens, for about 15 more minutes.

Immediately ladle chutney into hot sterilized ½-pint canning jars to within ¼ inch of rims. Wipe rims clean; top with scalded lids, then screw on bands. Let cool; test for a seal. Store in a cool, dark place. Makes 4½ pints.

Eggs & Cheese

International flavors, high protein power

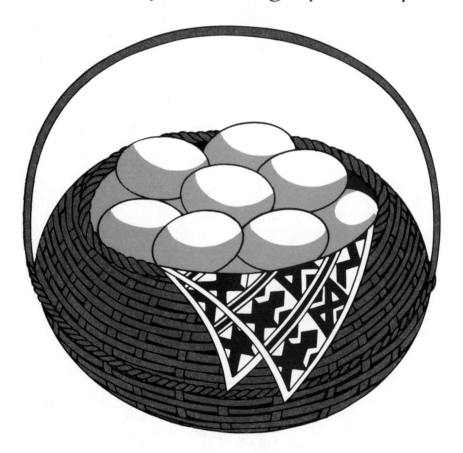

After cheese omelets, what? You'd be surprised—in the quest for distinctive and nutritious vegetarian entrées, eggs and cheese come up winners again and again. Or maybe it's not such a surprise. These two foods, both excellent protein sources, are easy to work with and adaptable to many different recipes. Individually or in tandem, they form the basis of some of the world's most celebrated meatless dishes.

Picture a crowd of skiers gathered around a crackling fire after a day on the slopes. With long forks, they are spearing chunks of bread to dunk into a bubbling pot of melted cheese and wine. It's fondue—the hot, satisfying cheese dish of Swiss inspiration that has gained worldwide popularity. In this chapter, we present a Dutch variation on the Swiss theme, using Holland's Gouda cheese.

In sunny Mexico, a family is preparing for supper. On the menu is tortilla hash, a mixture of corn tortilla pieces and eggs, with cheese melting over the top; it's served with sour cream and a zingy green sauce made from *tomatillos* (Mexican green tomatoes). You can offer this dish to your family, too, no matter how distant your home from the Mexican border.

In many other lands around the globe, dishes containing eggs and cheese are eagerly consumed. In Japan, we found a kind of savory main-dish custard; in France, the elegant, showy soufflé; and in Italy, the versatile frittata. Even scrambled eggs can be dressed up with other ingredients to adopt an ethnic personality—for example, Basque Scrambled Eggs flavored with garlic and olive oil, tomatoes and green pepper, for a bit of Spanish spirit.

Baked Eggplant Frittata

Italy

A frittata is an omelet, Italian-style—instead of filling and folding it, you stir the ingredients together and cook on both sides. You can accomplish this on the stove, but if you do it in the oven, the frittata puffs up to an airy lightness as it browns.

- ¼ cup olive oil or salad oil
- 1 small, unpeeled eggplant (about 1 lb.), cut into ½-inch cubes
- 1 medium-size onion, finely chopped
- 1 clove garlic, minced or pressed
- 3 large mushrooms, sliced
- 1 small zucchini, thinly sliced
- ¾ teaspoon *each* dry basil and oregano leaves
- ½ teaspoon salt
- ⅛ teaspoon pepper
- 3 large tomatoes (about 1¼ lbs. *total*), peeled, seeded, and chopped
- 4 eggs
- ½ cup grated Parmesan cheese
- 2 cups (8 oz.) shredded fontina or jack cheese Paprika

Heat oil in a wide frying pan over medium heat; add eggplant, onion, and garlic. Cook, stirring often, until vegetables are soft (about 10 minutes). Add mushrooms, zucchini, basil, oregano, salt, and pepper. Cook, stirring, until mushrooms are soft (about 7 more minutes). Add tomatoes and cook, stirring often until liquid evaporates (about 15 more minutes). Remove from heat and let mixture cool for about 15 minutes.

Meanwhile, in a small bowl, lightly beat eggs, add ¼ cup of the Parmesan cheese, then stir mixture into vegetables. Pour half of the vegetable-egg mixture into a well-greased 10-inch pie pan (1¾ inches deep) or an 8-inch-square baking dish. Top with 1 cup of the fontina cheese and the remaining vegetable-egg mixture. Sprinkle with remaining Parmesan and fontina cheeses, then lightly with paprika. Bake in a 400° oven (375° if in a glass container) for 25 to 30 minutes or until puffed and browned. Let cool on a rack for about 10 minutes before cutting. Makes 4 to 6 servings.

Artichoke & Feta Omelet

Greece

Feta, the tangy Greek cheese made from sheep's or goat's milk and pickled in brine, gives this omelet an assertive flavor. For a complete meal, serve the omelet with a green salad and crusty bread.

- 2 tablespoons butter or margarine
- 1 package (9 oz.) frozen artichoke hearts, thawed, drained, and quartered
- ⅓ cup finely chopped onion
- 1 tablespoon finely chopped parsley
- ½ teaspoon oregano leaves
- 2 tablespoons olive oil
- 8 eggs
- ¼ teaspoon salt
- ⅛ teaspoon pepper
- ⅓ cup (2 oz.) crumbled feta cheese
- 1 small tomato, thinly sliced

Melt butter in a wide frying pan over medium heat; add artichoke hearts, onion, parsley, and oregano and cook, stirring, until onion is soft (3 to 5 minutes). Drizzle oil over artichokes.

In a large bowl, beat eggs with salt and pepper. Pour egg mixture evenly over artichoke mixture. Cover, reduce heat to low, and cook for 3 minutes. Sprinkle with cheese and continue cooking, covered, until top is softly set but still moist and creamy (6 to 8 more minutes).

With a spatula, loosen edge, lift and slide half of the omelet onto a warm serving platter, then quickly flip pan so omelet folds onto itself on plate. Garnish with tomato slices. Serve immediately. Makes 4 servings.

Cheese & Vegetable Omelet

France

Country French cooks combine self-sufficiency and a love of good food in their cooking, with delicious results—witness this *omelette aux legumes et fromage*. They might use freshly laid eggs, mushrooms gathered in the woods, and home-grown shallots and bell peppers. But even if you buy your ingredients at the supermarket, you're sure to enjoy this flavorful—and easy-to-make—main dish.

- Sautéed Onions, Peppers & Mushrooms (recipe follows)
- 12 eggs
- ¼ cup water
- ½ teaspoon salt
- ⅛ teaspoon *each* ground nutmeg and white pepper
- 4 tablespoons butter or margarine
- 1 cup (4 oz.) shredded Gruyère or Swiss cheese Watercress sprigs

(Continued on page 59)

Prepare Sautéed Onions, Peppers & Mushrooms; set aside.

In a large bowl, beat eggs with water, salt, nutmeg, and pepper until well blended and frothy. In a 10 to 11-inch omelet pan or a nonstick frying pan with rounded sides, heat butter over medium-high heat until it begins to foam; tilt pan so butter coats bottom and sides. Pour in egg mixture.

Cook omelet, gently lifting cooked portion to let uncooked egg flow underneath. When top is softly set but still moist and creamy, sprinkle cheese in a strip down center in line with pan handle. Cover cheese with about a third of the sautéed vegetables.

To fold, tilt pan over a warm serving plate. With a spatula, fold top third of omelet over filling, then slide opposite third of omelet onto plate. Quickly flip pan so omelet folds onto itself on plate. Spoon remaining vegetables over omelet. Garnish with watercress sprigs. Makes 4 to 6 servings.

Sautéed Onions, Peppers & Mushrooms. Melt 4 tablespoons **butter** or margarine in a wide frying pan over medium heat. Add 1 medium-size **onion,** thinly sliced and separated into rings; 2 **shallots,** finely chopped; ½ pound **mushrooms,** thinly sliced; and 1 *each* **red and green bell pepper,** seeded and cut into thin strips. Cook, stirring occasionally, until mushrooms are lightly browned and liquid has evaporated. Season to taste with **salt** and **white pepper.**

Tortilla Hash with Green Sauce

Mexico

The Mexican name for this entrée of eggs, *tomatillos*, and shredded tortillas is *chilaquiles*, which, loosely translated, means "a broken-up old sombrero." A simple, informal dish, it was originally intended as a means of using up leftover or dried-out tortillas. Don't wait until you have leftovers, though—chilaquiles is worth making any time, for an easy and unusual brunch, lunch or supper.

The Basques, *over centuries of sheepherding, have developed virtuosity at campfire cooking. Here—adapted for kitchen cooking—are two spirited specialties: Basque Scrambled Eggs, glorified with tomatoes, green pepper, and robust seasonings (recipe on this page), to be served with light and crusty Sheepherder's Bread (page 84).*

8 six-inch Corn Tortillas (page 77 or purchased)
   Green Sauce (recipe follows)
5 tablespoons salad oil
1 small onion, finely chopped
8 eggs
½ cup milk
1 teaspoon oregano leaves
   Salt and pepper
2 cups (8 oz.) shredded jack cheese
   Mexican Cream (page 54) or sour cream
   Lime or lemon wedges

If tortillas are very fresh and moist, spread them out in a single layer and let stand for 1 to 2 hours to dry. Meanwhile, prepare Green Sauce and set aside. Cut tortillas in half, then into ½-inch-wide strips. Set aside.

Heat 2 tablespoons of the oil in a wide frying pan over medium heat. Add onion and cook, stirring, until soft. With a slotted spoon, transfer onions to a bowl and set aside. Pour remaining 3 tablespoons of oil into pan and increase heat to medium-high; add tortilla strips and cook, stirring, until pliable and firm but not crisp. Reduce heat to low.

In another bowl, beat eggs lightly with milk and oregano. Add egg mixture and onions to tortillas. Season to taste with salt and pepper. Cook, stirring gently, until eggs are softly set but still moist. Sprinkle with cheese, cover, and cook until cheese is melted (1 to 2 minutes). Serve immediately. Pass warm sauce, Mexican Cream, and lime wedges at table. Makes 6 servings.

Green Sauce. In a blender or food processor, combine 1 can (13 oz.) **Mexican green tomatoes** (*tomatillos*), well drained; 1 clove **garlic,** minced or pressed; ⅓ cup chopped fresh **coriander** (cilantro); and 1 small fresh, hot **green chile,** cored and seeded. Whirl until smooth. Season to taste with **salt.** Just before serving, heat sauce in a small pan over medium heat, stirring often, until heated through. Makes 1 cup.

Basque Scrambled Eggs

Spain   *Pictured on facing page*

High in the Pyrenees, which separate Spain from France, live the fiercely independent people called the Basques. They are a food-loving people, and their vibrant, colorful culture is reflected in dishes such as these scrambled eggs delectably embellished with garlic and herbs, tomatoes and green peppers.

(Continued on next page)

Eggs & Cheese 59

8 eggs
½ teaspoon salt
¼ teaspoon pepper
3 tablespoons olive oil
1 large onion, finely chopped
1 large green pepper, seeded and chopped
2 cloves garlic, minced or pressed
2 large tomatoes, peeled and chopped
2 canned pimentos, drained and chopped
1 teaspoon marjoram leaves
  Finely chopped parsley

In a medium-size bowl, beat eggs lightly with salt and pepper and set aside. Heat oil in a wide frying pan over medium heat. Add onion, green pepper, and garlic and cook, stirring, until onion is soft. Add tomatoes, pimentos, and marjoram; cook, stirring often, for 5 minutes. Add egg mixture and reduce heat to low; stir gently until cooked to your liking. Sprinkle with parsley. Makes 4 to 6 servings.

Egg Foo Yung

China

A traditional symbol of good luck in China—and a popular ingredient in Chinese cooking—is the egg. Chinese cooks use duck eggs, goose eggs, quail eggs, and squab eggs as well as those from chickens.

The Chinese egg dish perhaps best known to American palates is egg foo yung. This Cantonese specialty consists of golden-fried egg-patties, crunchy with vegetables and topped with soy-flavored foo yung sauce.

About 4 tablespoons salad oil
1 clove garlic, minced or pressed
1 medium-size carrot, shredded (about ½ cup)
2 green onions (including tops), thinly sliced
2 cups bean sprouts
  Foo Yung Sauce (recipe follows)
6 eggs
¾ teaspoon salt
⅛ teaspoon white pepper

Heat 2 tablespoons of the oil in a wide frying pan over medium-high heat; add garlic and carrot and cook, stirring, until carrots are tender-crisp (1 to 2 minutes). Stir in onions, then remove from heat and mix in bean sprouts; set aside.

Prepare Foo Yung Sauce; keep warm while preparing egg patties.

In a medium-size bowl, beat eggs with salt and

pepper. Stir in carrot mixture. Heat 2 more tablespoons of the oil in same frying pan over medium-high heat. Spoon in ¼ cup of the egg mixture for each patty, making 3 or 4 at a time. When egg is set, turn to cook other side until golden.

Transfer patties to a heated platter and keep warm. Repeat until all patties have been cooked, adding more oil to pan if needed. Pour Foo Yung Sauce over patties and serve at once. Makes 4 servings (8 patties).

Foo Yung Sauce. In a small pan, heat 1 cup **Root Vegetable Stock** (page 33), 1 tablespoon **soy sauce**, 2 teaspoons **sugar**, and 2 teaspoons **rice vinegar** or white wine vinegar over medium-high heat. In a small bowl, blend 1 tablespoon **cornstarch** with 2 tablespoons **water** and add to sauce. Cook, stirring, until sauce boils and thickens. Keep hot. Makes about 1 cup.

Egg-topped Potato Cakes with Peanut Sauce

Ecuador

Three mainstays of the Ecuadorian diet—potatoes, nuts, and eggs—are imaginatively combined in that country's well-known supper dish, *llapingachos*. To prepare this satisfying entrée, you fry individual mashed-potato cakes filled with cheese, top each with a fried or poached egg, and serve with warm peanut sauce.

Whipped Potato Cakes (recipe follows)
3 tablespoons butter or margarine
2 large onions, chopped
¼ cup creamy or crunchy peanut butter
½ cup Root Vegetable Stock (page 33), heated
  Salted peanuts, chopped
  Lettuce leaves
4 poached or fried eggs

Prepare Whipped Potato Cakes and keep warm.

Melt butter in a wide frying pan over medium heat. Add onions and cook, stirring often, until very soft and golden (about 30 minutes). Reduce heat to low and stir in peanut butter. Stirring, pour in stock slowly and stir until sauce is smooth. Transfer to a serving bowl and keep warm; garnish with peanuts.

To serve, place each potato cake on a lettuce-lined plate; top each with an egg. Pass peanut sauce at the table to spoon over individual servings. Makes 4 servings.

Whipped Potato Cakes. In a bowl, combine 2 to 2½ cups cold **mashed potatoes; 2 green onions** (including tops), finely chopped; and 2 tablespoons chopped **parsley.** Stir in 1 **egg yolk,** blending well. Slice about 1 ounce of **jack cheese** into 4 rectangles, each about ½ inch thick. Divide potato mixture into 4 equal portions and shape each around a piece of cheese, forming a patty about 1 inch thick. Lightly coat both sides of each patty with **yellow cornmeal.**

Melt 3 tablespoons **butter** or margarine in a wide frying pan over medium heat. Add potato cakes and cook until well browned on both sides (about 8 minutes *total*), turning cakes carefully with a wide spatula. Makes 4 cakes.

Steamed Vegetable Custard

Japan

For cooking their custards, the Japanese make special ceramic cups shaped like western custard cups but taller and with loose-fitting lids. But you can use large coffee cups or mugs, regular custard cups, or any heat-resistant dishes that will hold about 8 ounces.

    8 Chinese edible-pod peas, or ¼ cup fresh or
       frozen shelled peas, thawed
    1 medium-size carrot, thinly sliced
    ½ cup thinly sliced mushrooms
    2 cups Root Vegetable Stock (page 33)
    6 eggs
    2 teaspoons soy sauce
    1 teaspoon *each* sherry (optional) and sugar
    ¼ teaspoon salt
       Sesame oil or salad oil
    2 or 3 leaves spinach, shredded, or 12 small
       watercress sprigs
    6 thin slices fresh ginger or 3 paper-thin lemon
       slices, halved

Bring 3 inches of water to a boil in a 2-quart pan over high heat; add edible-pod peas and cook just until water again comes to a boil (about 30 seconds). With a slotted spoon, remove peas; cut crosswise into ¼-inch-wide strips. (If using fresh or frozen shelled peas, no precooking is necessary.) Add carrot to cooking liquid and bring to a boil; continue boiling until tender-crisp (2 to 3 minutes). Remove with a slotted spoon; discard cooking liquid. In a small bowl, combine sliced pea pods, carrot, and mushrooms; set aside.

In pan, bring Root Vegetable Stock to steaming over high heat; remove from heat. In a large bowl, beat eggs with soy, sherry, sugar, and salt until blended. Slowly pour in stock, beating.

Oil six 8-ounce bowls. Distribute vegetable mixture and spinach evenly among bowls; pour in egg mixture and stir gently with a fork. Place a slice of ginger in center of each.

Cover loosely with wax paper or foil and place on a rack over ½ inch of hot water in an electric frying pan with domed lid or in a covered roasting pan. Bring water to a boil over high heat, then adjust heat to keep it boiling gently. Cover pan and cook until custards are just softly set (8 to 12 minutes—time varies depending on shape and thickness of cooking dishes).

To test doneness, insert a metal spoon about ½ inch into center of custard; if set, custard will break and a little clear liquid may flow into the depression. Serve hot. Makes 6 servings.

Bernese Onion Tart

Switzerland

This tart, made with sautéed onions and Swiss cheese, is inspired by the onion festival held each November in Bern.

       Flaky Pastry (recipe follows)
    3 tablespoons butter or margarine
    5 or 6 medium-size onions, thinly sliced
       (2½ lbs. *total*)
    ¼ cup unbleached all-purpose flour
    ½ teaspoon salt
    ⅛ teaspoon ground nutmeg
    1 teaspoon dry mustard
    1 cup milk
    3 eggs
    ½ pint (1 cup) sour cream
    2 cups (8 oz.) shredded Swiss, Gruyère, or
       Emmenthaler cheese
       Salt

Prepare Flaky Pastry and set aside.

Melt butter in a 3 to 4-quart pan over medium heat. Add onions and cook, covered, stirring often, until soft (10 to 15 minutes). Uncover and continue cooking, stirring often, until lightly browned (10 to 12 more minutes).

Stir in flour, salt, nutmeg, and mustard. Remove from heat and slowly pour in milk, stirring. Return to heat and bring to a boil, stirring; continue boiling and stirring until sauce thickens. Set aside.

In a large bowl, beat eggs until blended, then mix in sour cream and cheese. Stir onion mixture into sour cream mixture; season to taste with salt.

On a floured board, roll out pastry to form a circle about 12 inches in diameter; fit dough into a

10-inch pie plate and fold excess under; flute edge. Pour in filling. Bake on bottom rack of a 350° oven for 55 minutes or until crust is browned and filling is firm when plate is gently shaken. Let cool on a rack for 5 to 10 minutes before cutting into wedges to serve. Makes 8 servings.

Flaky Pastry. In a medium-size bowl, mix 1½ cups **unbleached all-purpose flour** and ¼ teaspoon **salt**. With a pastry blender or 2 knives, cut in 6 tablespoons firm **butter** or margarine and 2 tablespoons **solid shortening** until mixture resembles coarse crumbs. In a small bowl, beat 1 **egg** with 1 tablespoon **water**. Slowly pour egg mixture into flour mixture, stirring. Continue stirring until mixture is evenly moistened and begins to hold together. Shape dough into a ball and flatten. If made ahead, wrap and refrigerate until the next day. Bring to room temperature before using.

Spinach & Cheese Soufflé

Luxembourg   *Pictured on facing page*

Perhaps no dish represents classic French cuisine better than the soufflé; its very name, which in French means "breath," conveys its light and ephemeral elegance. Though French in origin, the soufflé has relatives in other countries—such as this spinach and cheese version from Luxembourg.

> 3 tablespoons butter or margarine
> 3 tablespoons unbleached all-purpose flour
> ½ teaspoon *each* salt and dry tarragon
> ⅛ teaspoon ground nutmeg
> 1 cup milk
> 1 cup (4 oz.) shredded Swiss cheese
> 6 eggs, separated
> ½ cup cooked, squeezed, and chopped spinach
> Butter or margarine

Preheat oven to 375°

Melt the 3 tablespoons butter in a 3-quart pan over medium heat; stir in flour, salt, tarragon, and nutmeg and cook until bubbly. Stirring, pour in milk slowly; cook, stirring, until mixture boils and thickens. Add cheese and stir until melted. Remove from heat and stir in egg yolks, one at a time; mix until well blended. Stir in spinach; set aside.

Beat egg whites until soft, moist peaks form. Fold half of the beaten whites into cheese mixture; then fold in the remaining whites. Pour into a well-buttered 2-quart soufflé dish. Bake for 30 to 35 minutes or until soufflé is golden and feels firm when lightly tapped. Serve immediately. Makes 4 or 5 servings.

Garlic Soufflé

United States

The little town of Gilroy, California, calls itself "The Garlic Capital of the World," and for good reason, for it is here that much of the world's garlic is grown. Each summer the town holds a garlic festival, at which the public is offered a chance to celebrate the harvest by sampling some special dishes made with garlic—such as this soufflé. Don't be scared off by its name; it is unmistakably garlicky, but surprisingly mild in flavor.

> 4 tablespoons butter or margarine
> 2 tablespoons grated Parmesan cheese
> 3 cloves garlic, minced or pressed
> Dash *each* ground red pepper (cayenne) and ground nutmeg
> ¼ teaspoon *each* salt and dry mustard
> 3 tablespoons unbleached all-purpose flour
> 1 cup milk
> 1 cup (4 oz.) shredded jack cheese
> 5 eggs, separated

Preheat oven to 375°.

Coat bottom and sides of a 2-quart soufflé dish with 1 tablespoon of the butter, then with the Parmesan cheese; set dish aside.

Melt remaining 3 tablespoons butter in a 3-quart pan over low heat. Add garlic and cook, stirring occasionally, until garlic is soft and golden but not browned (about 5 minutes). Stir in red pepper, nutmeg, salt, mustard, and flour. Cook over medium heat, stirring, until bubbly. Remove from heat and pour in milk slowly, stirring. Return to heat and cook, stirring, until mixture boils and thickens. Add the jack cheese and stir until melted. Remove from heat and mix in egg yolks, one at a time; stir until well blended.

Beat egg whites until soft, moist peaks form. Fold half of the beaten whites into cheese mixture; then fold in the remaining whites. Pour mixture into prepared soufflé dish. Bake for 25 to 30 minutes or until soufflé is golden and feels firm when lightly tapped. Serve immediately. Makes 4 servings.

A billow of cheese and spinach, *this golden soufflé (recipe on this page) comes from tiny Luxembourg, where people enjoy the culinary influence of neighboring France. Sink your teeth into a slice of the Whole Wheat Baguettes (page 83) for a contrasting texture.*

Making Protein-rich Fresh Cheese

For centuries, making fresh cheese at home has been a custom in many cultures, and it's not nearly as complicated as you might think. The two cheese recipes that follow require no special equipment, and they produce fresh cheeses that are tasty, healthful, and versatile.

The first recipe is for Milk Cheese, known in India as *paneer*. Made of boiling milk clotted with lemon juice, it is a slightly tangy white cheese. It's used in the recipes for traditional Indian dishes represented here and on page 13.

Our Yogurt Cheese is similar to Israeli *lebineeya*, a thick, flavorful cheese. Here, it's an ingredient in the Indian recipe for Yogurt Cheese Omelet and in Yogurt Cheese Spread, a version of the Hungarian Liptauer spread.

Milk Cheese (*Pictured on page 19*). Combine 2 quarts **whole milk** and ½ teaspoon **salt** (optional) in a deep, heavy 6 to 8-quart kettle. Bring to a boil over medium-high heat, stirring occasionally (15 to 20 minutes). Bottom of kettle may become scorched, but this will not affect cheese. Stir in ⅓ cup **lemon juice** (curd will separate from whey quickly). Continue boiling for 2 more minutes, without stirring (milk will froth); then remove from heat.

Line a colander with clean cheesecloth (large enough to hang over sides) that has been dipped in cold water and wrung dry. Pour mixture into colander. (If making Milk Cheese to use in the following Indian recipes, place colander over a container to catch whey.) Let cheese drain until most of whey is gone (about 5 minutes). Scrape cheese toward center.

To finish making cheese, drain or press it as follows:

For drained cheese, twist together corners of cheesecloth to wrap cheese tightly. Turn over in colander; let drain at room temperature for 20 minutes.

For pressed cheese, fold cheesecloth securely over cheese to enclose, then invert onto a 10 by 15-inch rimmed baking pan. Place a 4 to 5-quart kettle filled with water on wrapped cheese; let stand for about 30 minutes. Lift pan off cheese and unwrap; discard drained liquid.

To store, wrap airtight and refrigerate for up to 2 weeks. Makes 1¼ cups.

Yogurt Cheese (*Pictured on page 66*). Line a colander with a clean cheesecloth (20 inches square) that has been dipped in cold water and wrung dry. Pour in 2 pints (4 cups) **plain yogurt**. Fold cloth over yogurt and twist ends to enclose. Place colander in a larger bowl and let yogurt drain at room temperature for 3 to 5 hours. Refrigerate until next day. Yogurt cheese will have a thick, creamy consistency. Unwrap and invert onto a serving plate or scoop into another container. To store, cover and refrigerate for up to 1 week. Discard clear yellow liquid drained from yogurt. Makes 1½ to 2 cups cheese.

Cheese with Spinach

- 1 pound spinach
- 1 tablespoon butter or margarine
- 1 tablespoon salad oil
- ½ teaspoon cumin seeds
- 1 large onion, finely chopped
- 2 large cloves garlic, minced or pressed
- 1 large tomato, chopped
- 1 small fresh, hot green chile, seeded and finely chopped (optional)
- 1 teaspoon ground coriander
- ½ teaspoon turmeric
- ¼ teaspoon ground red pepper (cayenne)
- 1 cup reserved whey or water
  Salt
- 1¼ cups pressed Milk Cheese (recipe on this page), cut into ½-inch cubes
- 8 to 10 Flour Tortillas with Sesame Seeds (page 77 or purchased flour tortillas), or 4 pocket breads
- ½ pint (1 cup) plain yogurt
- ⅓ cup chopped almonds

Remove and discard tough spinach stems; rinse leaves well. Place leaves, with water that clings to them, in a 3 to 4-quart pan. Cover and cook over medium heat, stirring occasionally, until spinach is wilted (about 7 minutes). Transfer to a blender or food processor and whirl until puréed; set aside.

Heat butter and oil in a wide frying pan over medium-high heat. Add cumin and cook, stirring, until lightly toasted (about 30 seconds). Add onion and garlic and cook, stirring, until onions are lightly browned (about 10 more minutes). Stir in tomato, chile (if desired), coriander, turmeric, and red pepper. Cook, stirring, until tomato is very soft (about 10 more minutes).

Add whey and bring to a boil over high heat. Stirring, continue boiling until sauce is well combined (3 to 5 minutes). Season to taste with salt. Reduce heat to low, stir in puréed spinach, then gently mix in cheese. Cook, uncovered, until cheese is heated through (about 1 minute).

Serve immediately (spinach discolors if held on heat). Serve with warm tortillas, or spoon into warm pocket bread. Top with yogurt and almonds. Makes 4 servings.

Cheese Curry

    1 tablespoon butter or margarine
    1 tablespoon salad oil
    1 large onion, finely chopped
    4 large cloves garlic, minced or pressed
    2 teaspoons finely chopped fresh ginger
    2 medium-size tomatoes, chopped
    1 teaspoon *each* cumin seeds, ground coriander, and turmeric
    ¼ to ½ teaspoon ground red pepper (cayenne)
    ¼ teaspoon fennel seeds, crushed
    1½ cups reserved whey or water
    1 tablespoon chopped fresh coriander (cilantro) or parsley
      Salt
    3 cups hot cooked rice (page 45)
    1¼ cups pressed Milk Cheese (recipe on facing page), cut into ½-inch cubes
    ⅓ cup coarsely chopped salted cashews

Heat butter and oil in a wide frying pan over medium-high heat. Add onion, garlic, and ginger and cook, stirring, until onions are lightly browned (about 10 minutes). Add tomatoes, cumin, the ground coriander, turmeric, red pepper, and fennel. Cook, stirring, until tomatoes no longer hold their shape (about 10 minutes).

Stir in whey and bring to a boil over high heat. Continue boiling, stirring, until sauce is well combined (3 to 5 minutes). Mix in the chopped coriander; season to taste with salt. Cover, reduce heat, and simmer for 20 minutes.

Meanwhile, prepare rice.

Gently stir cheese into sauce. Cook, covered, until cheese is heated through (about 3 minutes). To serve, spoon curry over rice and top with cashews. Makes 4 servings.

Yogurt Cheese Spread

    ½ cup (¼ lb.) butter or margarine, softened
    1 cup Yogurt Cheese (recipe on facing page)
    1 teaspoon caraway seeds
    ¾ teaspoon sweet Hungarian paprika
    ¼ teaspoon dry mustard
    ⅛ teaspoon black pepper
    1 tablespoon *each* chopped capers and minced chives
      Salt
      Rye or wheat crackers, or thinly sliced pumpernickel bread

In a medium-size bowl, cream butter until fluffy. Add yogurt cheese slowly, beating; continue beating until well blended. Stir in caraway seeds, paprika, mustard, and pepper; then add capers and chives. Season to taste with salt. Cover and refrigerate for 3 to 4 hours to blend flavors. Let stand at room temperature for about 30 minutes before serving. Spread on crackers. To store, cover and refrigerate for up to 1 week. Makes about 1⅔ cups.

Yogurt Cheese Omelet

    1 tablespoon butter or margarine
    1 green onion (including top), finely chopped
    2 eggs, lightly beaten
    1 tablespoon diced canned green chiles
      Salt and pepper
    3 tablespoons Yogurt Cheese (recipe on facing page)
      Dash *each* curry powder and ground cumin

Melt butter in an 8-inch omelet pan over medium-high heat. Add onion and cook, stirring, for 1 minute. Pour in eggs and sprinkle evenly with chiles; season to taste with salt and pepper. Cook omelet, gently lifting cooked portion to let uncooked egg flow underneath. When top of omelet is softly set but still moist and creamy, spoon yogurt cheese in a strip down center in line with pan handle. Sprinkle with curry powder and cumin.

To fold, tilt pan over a warm serving plate. With a spatula, fold top third of omelet over filling, then slide opposite third of omelet onto plate. Quickly flip pan so omelet folds onto itself on plate. Makes 1 serving.

Pizza Turnovers

Italy

In Italy, these plump, crusty turnovers are known as *calzone*, which actually means "trouser legs." Rest assured, though, that their pizza-style filling gives them a much more appealing flavor than a pair of pants could ever hope to achieve!

Crusty Dough (recipe follows)
About 3 tablespoons olive oil
 1 small onion, sliced
 1 clove garlic, minced or pressed
 ½ pound mushrooms, sliced
 1 small green pepper, seeded and sliced
 1 small carrot, thinly sliced
 1 can (8 oz.) tomato sauce
 1 small can (2¼ oz.) sliced ripe olives, drained
 1 teaspoon *each* dry basil and oregano leaves
 ½ teaspoon sugar
 ½ teaspoon fennel seeds (optional)
 ¼ teaspoon crushed red pepper
 2½ cups (10 oz.) shredded mozzarella cheese
 ¾ cup grated Parmesan cheese
Salt and pepper
Cornmeal

Prepare Crusty Dough. While it rises, prepare filling. Heat 3 tablespoons of the oil in a wide frying pan over medium heat. Add onion, garlic, mushrooms, green pepper, and carrot. Cook, stirring, until vegetables are soft (6 to 8 minutes). Stir in tomato sauce, olives, basil, oregano, sugar, fennel seeds (if desired), and red pepper. Simmer, uncovered, for about 5 minutes. Let cool.

When ready to assemble turnovers, stir mozzarella and Parmesan cheeses into vegetable mixture. Season to taste with salt and pepper.

After dough rises, punch down and divide in half. On a lightly floured board, shape each portion into a ball, then roll each into an 11-inch circle. Lightly brush surface of each circle with olive oil.

Spread half the filling over half of a circle. Fold plain half over filling, then press edges together. Turn a ½-inch edge up and over, seal, and crimp. Repeat with remaining dough and filling. With a wide spatula, transfer turnovers to a greased and cornmeal-dusted baking sheet. With a fork, pierce tops in several places; brush lightly with olive oil.

Encircling a challah, *the traditional Jewish sabbath Egg Bread (page 84), are the all-fresh foods of a typical Israeli breakfast: shredded carrots (to be sprinkled with orange juice), tomato wedges, hard-cooked eggs, cucumber slices, olives, fresh fruit, and Yogurt Cheese (page 64).*

Bake in a 475° oven for 15 to 20 minutes or until well browned. Makes 4 servings (2 large turnovers).

Crusty Dough. In a bowl, dissolve 1 package **active dry yeast** in 1 cup warm **water** (about 110°) and let stand until bubbly (5 to 15 minutes). Stir in ½ teaspoon **salt** and 2 teaspoons **olive oil** or salad oil. Mix in 2½ to 3 cups **unbleached all-purpose flour** to make a soft dough. Turn dough out onto a well-floured board and knead until smooth and not sticky, adding more flour if needed. Place in a greased bowl; turn dough over to grease top. Cover and let rise in a warm place until doubled (about 1 hour).

Gouda Fondue

Holland

Fondue is a Swiss idea, and usually it's made with Emmenthaler or Gruyère cheese. Our recipe, though, is Dutch, and uses Holland's Gouda cheese for a delicious flavor variation. Even so, you might take a tip from the fondue experts of Switzerland, who insist that the cook must stir with a wooden fork in a figure-eight pattern when blending the cheese into the fondue.

 1 clove garlic, halved
 1½ cups dry white wine
 4 cups (1 lb.) shredded Gouda cheese
 1 teaspoon Dijon mustard
 1 tablespoon potato flour or cornstarch
 2 tablespoons kirsch (optional)
Freshly ground nutmeg and white pepper
About 8 thick slices fresh whole-grain bread or French bread, cut into bite-size cubes

Rub the inside of a heavy 2-quart pan with garlic. Add wine and cook over medium-low heat until bubbles rise slowly to the surface. Meanwhile, in a bowl, lightly mix cheese, mustard, and flour.

Stir cheese mixture into wine, a spoonful at a time. Continue stirring slowly until mixture is smooth (it should bubble slowly). Add kirsch, if desired, 1 tablespoon at a time and again bring fondue to a simmer (too-high heat may cause fondue to separate).

To serve, transfer fondue to a chafing dish over an alcohol burner or to a serving dish on an electric warmer. Season to taste with nutmeg and pepper. Adjust heat so fondue keeps bubbling *slowly*. Offer fondue forks or bamboo skewers to spear bread for dipping into fondue. Makes 4 entrée servings or 10 to 12 appetizer servings.

Pancake, Crêpe & Tortilla Entrées

Fill-and-wrap breads from near and far

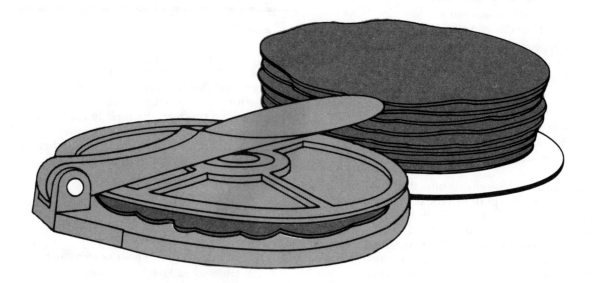

It is for good reason that, in cuisines the world over, there exists that flat and flexible creation we call the pancake. Because of its seemingly endless versatility, this basic food has become an almost universal culinary standby.

Consider the crêpe, for example. This light and delicate French specialty is the aristocrat of pancakes. What could be more elegant than a supper of tender crêpes wrapped around a creamy mushroom filling accented with sherry?

Conversely, consider the tortilla. This earthy breadlike pancake is a staple food of Mexico, and appears in and alongside many Mexican meals, usually as part of a spicy, robust menu.

The same type of pancake can even assume a double role—in either a simple meal or an elegant one. Blini, the Russian version of pancakes, are the basis of one of the world's grand dishes when topped with sour cream and caviar and enjoyed with a glass of ice-cold vodka. But topped with chopped egg and onions, blini become a hearty and delicious peasant food.

Humble or highbrow, the pancake's variations in flavor, texture, and function are nothing short of astonishing. Pancakes may be made with grains ranging from corn to buckwheat, or completely without grains—just with eggs. They may be made to rise with yeast or with baking powder, or not at all. And they may be baked or fried, folded or rolled, filled or topped—or just eaten alone.

Pancakes and their relatives may appear at the table at every meal and from appetizer to dessert. Here, though, we concentrate on pancakes as entrées. In all their forms, these flat, soft breads are beautifully suited for use in main dishes for vegetarian dining.

Dinner Pancakes with Seasoned Vegetables

Ethiopia

The staple food of Ethiopia—a large, round pancake called *injera*—functions at mealtime as both a plate and a scooper. To serve it with seasoned vegetables, have each guest place a pancake on a dinner plate and pile vegetables on top. Spoon a dollop of yogurt or—to be more nearly authentic—cottage cheese atop the vegetables. Extra pancakes are torn apart and used to scoop up or wrap around bites of the vegetables. If you like, you can offer knives and forks, but the traditional Ethiopian eating utensils are merely the fingers of the right hand.

Dinner Pancakes (recipe follows)
1 pound *each* carrots, tiny red new potatoes, and broccoli
1 small head cauliflower (about 1 lb.)
About 4 tablespoons butter or margarine
¼ teaspoon *each* ground cinnamon, ground cardamom, and ground ginger
⅛ teaspoon *each* ground cloves and turmeric
2 cloves garlic, minced or pressed
1 large onion, finely chopped
Salt
Plain yogurt or cottage cheese

Prepare Dinner Pancakes.

Cut carrots into ¼-inch-thick slices. Scrub potatoes (if larger than bite-size, cut into quarters). Cut flowerets off broccoli stalks. Cut off and discard tough base of stalks, peel stalks, and cut into ¼-inch-thick slices. Break cauliflower into flowerets. Cut larger broccoli flowerets and cauliflowerets in half lengthwise.

Arrange potatoes in a vegetable steamer; steam over boiling water until tender (about 15 minutes); remove potatoes and let cool. Add water to steamer, if needed. Arrange carrots, broccoli stems, and cauliflowerets in steamer; steam until just tender (about 9 minutes). Add broccoli flowerets; steam until tender (about 1½ more minutes). (At this point, you may let cool, cover, and refrigerate for 4 to 6 hours.)

Melt 4 tablespoons of the butter in a wide frying pan over medium heat. Stir in cinnamon, cardamom, ginger, cloves, turmeric, garlic, and onion. Cook, stirring, until onion is soft; then stir in carrots, broccoli stems, cauliflowerets, and potatoes. Cook, covered, stirring often, for about 7 minutes. Add butter if needed, then add broccoli flowerets. Cook, covered, until flowerets are heated through (about 4 more minutes). Season to taste with salt. Pass yogurt at the table. Makes 4 to 6 servings.

Dinner Pancakes. Pour 1 cup warm **water** (about 110°) into a blender or food processor; sprinkle 3 packages **active dry yeast** over water. Add 3 cups **buttermilk baking mix**, 1½ cups warm **milk** (about 110°), 3 **eggs**, and ⅓ cup **butter** or margarine, melted and cooled. Whirl until batter is smooth.

Place a 7 to 8-inch crêpe pan, omelet pan, or other flat-bottomed frying pan over medium-low to medium heat. When hot, add about ¼ teaspoon **butter** or margarine and swirl pan to coat bottom. Pour in ⅓ cup batter all at once and rotate pan so batter covers bottom. Cook until top looks dry. With a wide spatula, flip pancake; cook until browned on other side, then transfer to a plate.

Repeat with remaining batter (pancakes may be stacked). If made ahead, let cool, wrap, and refrigerate for up to 2 days. Bring to room temperature before separating. Makes 18 pancakes.

Blini

Russia

During *Maslenitsa* (the week-long "Butter Festival" that traditionally precedes Russia's Lenten season) you might dine on *blini* by the dozen at every meal. Invented by early Slavs to represent the sun they worshiped at the spring equinox, the miniature pancake rose to aristocratic grandeur in Czarist Russia when it was topped with beluga caviar and sour cream. The common-folk's toppings—chopped eggs, sliced onions, sour cream, and dill—are just as exquisite, in both appearance and taste.

⅔ cup milk
1 package active dry yeast
¼ cup warm water (about 110°)
1 teaspoon sugar
⅔ cup unbleached all-purpose flour
¼ cup buckwheat pancake mix
¼ teaspoon salt
2 eggs, separated
3 tablespoons sour cream
Butter
Toppings (suggestions follow)

Bring milk to scalding in a small pan over medium heat; let cool. In a large bowl, combine yeast, water, and sugar; let stand until bubbly (5 to 15 minutes). In another bowl, combine flour, pancake mix, and salt; then add to yeast mixture along with milk, egg yolks, and sour cream. Beat until smooth and well blended (about 3 minutes). Cover and let stand at room temperature until mixture is spongy and has a slightly sour smell (about 4 hours).

In a bowl, beat egg whites until soft, moist peaks form. Gently fold into batter; let stand for 30 minutes.

Heat a griddle or wide frying pan over medium-high heat; brush lightly with butter. Ladle 3 tablespoons batter onto griddle for each pancake; cook until tops are dry and bubbles break (about 3 minutes). Turn and brown other side. Stack pancakes and keep them warm while preparing remaining pancakes. Pass toppings at the table. Makes 4 servings (16 pancakes).

Toppings. Offer ½ cup (¼ lb.) **butter**, melted; ½ pint (1 cup) **sour cream**; 1 **mild red onion**, thinly sliced; 4 **hard-cooked eggs**, chopped; and fresh or dry **dill weed**.

Mandarin Pancakes with Spicy Tofu Filling

China   *Pictured on facing page*

Peking's contribution to the world's pancake stack functions like a tortilla—as a hand-held edible wrapper. Whether rolled around our spicy Oriental filling or any other of your liking, it's as delicate and delicious as a crêpe, but slightly puffier. You can prepare the pancakes a few days ahead and refrigerate, or a few weeks ahead and freeze.

          Mandarin Pancakes (recipe follows)
          Spicy Sauce (recipe follows)
    3 tablespoons salad oil
    1 medium-size onion, finely chopped
    1 cup thinly sliced celery
    1½ cups chopped broccoli
    2 cups thinly sliced mushrooms
    2½ cups diced medium-firm tofu
    1½ cups bean sprouts

Prepare Mandarin Pancakes and Spicy Sauce.

Heat oil in a wide frying pan over medium heat. Add onion and celery and cook, stirring often, for 3 to 4 minutes. Add broccoli; cook, stirring, for 2 to 3 more minutes. Stir in mushrooms; continue cooking, stirring, until liquid has evaporated and mushrooms are soft. Add tofu and mix lightly until heated through. Stir in Spicy Sauce.

Just before filling pancakes, stir bean sprouts into vegetables and heat through.

Spoon an equal amount of filling down center of each pancake. Roll up to eat out of hand. Makes 6 servings.

Mandarin Pancakes. In a bowl, mix 1½ cups **unbleached all-purpose flour** and ½ cup **whole wheat flour** (not stone-ground). Add ¾ cup boiling **water** and, with a fork, mix for several minutes until dough holds together. On a lightly floured board, knead until smooth and satiny (about 10 minutes). Cover and let stand at room temperature for 30 minutes.

Shape dough into a 12-inch-long log. Cut into 1-inch-thick slices and cover.

For each pancake, halve 1 piece of dough (keep remaining dough covered while preparing pancakes). Form each half into a ball, flatten slightly, and, with a rolling pin, roll on a lightly floured board to a circle 3 inches in diameter. Lightly brush **sesame oil** or salad oil on top of one circle and cover with the other (altogether you will need about 2 tablespoons oil). Press the rounds firmly together.

On a lightly floured board, roll the double circle from center to edges, forming a pancake 7 to 8 inches in diameter. Turn frequently, dusting board lightly with flour as needed. Repeat until you have 2 or 3 pancakes.

Heat an ungreased wide frying pan over medium-high heat. Place a pancake in pan. Turn about every 15 seconds until pancake becomes blistered by air pockets, turns parchment color, and feels dry. (Pancake should not brown, but a few brown spots won't hurt. If overcooked, pancake becomes brittle.)

Remove pancake from pan. Carefully pull apart the two halves and stack them on a plate. Keep covered as you shape and cook remaining pancakes. Serve warm; or let cool, wrap airtight, and refrigerate for up to 3 days. Freeze for longer storage.

To reheat, thaw if frozen. Line a flat-bottomed steamer with a towel dipped in water and wrung dry; stack pancakes inside and fold towel over pancakes. Cover and steam over simmering water for 5 minutes. Keep covered until ready to serve. Makes 24 pancakes.

Spicy Sauce. Stir together 5 tablespoons **soy sauce**; 3 tablespoons **cider vinegar**; 2 teaspoons **cornstarch**; 3 large cloves **garlic**, minced or pressed; 3 tablespoons chopped **fresh coriander** (cilantro); and ½ teaspoon crushed **small dried hot red chile**.

Spicy, exotic, *yet exquisitely simple, this Chinese supper presents a tempting tofu-vegetable filling to wrap inside Mandarin Pancakes (recipe on this page), warm from the steamer basket.*

Zucchini Pancakes

United States

As anyone knows who has grown zucchini, it tends toward exuberance. Necessity being the mother of invention, zucchini overload has led gardeners across the United States to come up with clever and delicious zucchini recipes. This one, a savory entrée pancake, makes a satisfying summertime supper with Garlic Cheese Bread (page 85) and a salad.

3 cups shredded zucchini (about 1¼ lbs. *total*)
⅓ cup minced onion
3 eggs, lightly beaten
¾ cup unbleached all-purpose flour
¾ teaspoon *each* baking powder and salt
¼ teaspoon pepper
½ teaspoon oregano leaves
   About ½ cup salad oil
   Grated Parmesan cheese (optional)

Squeeze zucchini firmly to remove excess liquid. Transfer to a bowl and mix with onion, eggs, flour,

The Versatile, Elegant Crêpe

The thought of making crêpes—an everyday standby in France—used to be intimidating to all but the French. With the right pan and a little practice, though, crêpes are surprisingly easy to make. You'll find that the recipes below give full, detailed directions on how to handle the thin batter successfully.

To an otherwise authentic basic batter, we've added sesame seeds for extra protein and a slight crunch. Next comes a whole wheat version for those who relish the more vigorous, slightly nutty flavor. And in yet another departure from French tradition, we offer a cornmeal soy variation—also richer in nutrients. All three wrap deliciously around savory fillings for supper, Sesame or Whole Wheat crêpes around preserves for dessert.

Sesame Crêpes

3 eggs
1 cup milk
1 tablespoon salad oil
⅔ cup unbleached all-purpose flour
¼ cup sesame seeds
⅛ teaspoon salt
   About 4 teaspoons salad oil

In a blender or food processor (or with a wire whisk, egg beater, or electric mixer), whirl eggs, milk, the 1 tablespoon oil, flour, sesame seeds, and

salt until smooth. Cover and refrigerate for 1 hour.

Heat a 6 or 7-inch crêpe pan or other flat-bottomed frying pan over medium heat. Pour in about ¼ teaspoon of the remaining 4 teaspoons oil and swirl to coat surface. When pan is sizzling hot (test with a few drops of water), pour in about 2 tablespoons of the batter all at once, tilting pan so batter flows quickly over entire flat surface. Cook until surface looks dry and edge is lightly browned. With a spatula, turn crêpe; cook other side until lightly browned.

Repeat with remaining batter, adding a little oil as needed to prevent crêpes from sticking. Stack crêpes on a plate as they are completed. If made ahead, place wax paper between crêpes, wrap airtight, and refrigerate for up to 3 days; freeze for longer storage. Bring crêpes to room temperature before separating. Fill crêpes as desired and roll or fold to serve. Makes 16 to 18 crêpes.

Whole Wheat Crêpes. Prepare **Sesame Crêpes,** but substitute ¾ cup **whole wheat flour** (not stone ground) for flour and sesame seeds. Makes 16 to 18 crêpes.

Cornmeal Soy Crêpes. Prepare **Sesame Crêpes,** but substitute ⅓ cup **yellow cornmeal,** ¼ cup **unbleached all-purpose flour,** and 2 tablespoons **soy flour** or soy powder for flour and sesame seeds. Stir batter often while preparing crêpes. Makes 16 to 18 crêpes.

baking powder, salt, pepper, and oregano; blend well.

Heat 2 tablespoons of the oil in a wide frying pan over medium-high heat. Add about 3 tablespoons of the zucchini mixture for each pancake; spread to make 4-inch circles. Cook 4 pancakes at a time, turning once, until golden brown on both sides (3 to 4 minutes per side). With a spatula, lift out pancakes; drain briefly on paper towels. Transfer to a serving platter and keep warm.

Repeat with remaining batter. Pass cheese to sprinkle over individual servings, if desired. Makes 4 servings (16 pancakes).

Spinach-Ricotta Crêpes

Italy

We've adapted one of Italy's favorite flavor combinations as a filling for crêpes. Nutrient-rich, emerald green spinach blends beautifully with creamy white ricotta cheese.

　　Fresh Tomato Sauce (recipe follows)
1　egg
½　teaspoon salt
⅛　teaspoon *each* pepper and ground nutmeg
2　cups (1 lb.) ricotta cheese
2　cups (8 oz.) shredded jack cheese
¾　cup grated Parmesan cheese
1　tablespoon chopped parsley
½　cup cooked, squeezed, and chopped spinach
16　to 18 Sesame Crêpes (page 72)
　　Chopped parsley

Prepare Fresh Tomato Sauce.

In a medium-size bowl, beat egg with salt, pepper, and nutmeg. Mix in ricotta cheese, jack cheese, ¼ cup of the Parmesan cheese, the 1 tablespoon parsley, and spinach. Spoon an equal amount of ricotta mixture down center of each crêpe; roll to enclose. Spoon about half the tomato sauce into a 9 by 13-inch baking dish. Place a single layer of filled crêpes, seam side down, in sauce. Cover with remaining sauce and sprinkle evenly with remaining ½ cup Parmesan cheese. Bake, uncovered, in a 350° oven for 25 to 30 minutes or until crêpes are heated through, cheese is browned, and sauce bubbles all over. Sprinkle with chopped parsley. Makes 4 to 6 servings.

Fresh Tomato Sauce. Remove stem and root ends from 1 large **onion;** cut in half lengthwise and thinly slice onion lengthwise so that it falls into slivers. Heat 3 tablespoons **olive oil** in a 2½ to 3-quart pan over medium heat; add onion and

cook, stirring, until soft but not browned. Mix in 1 small clove **garlic,** minced or pressed, and 1 medium-size **red bell pepper,** seeded and chopped; cook, stirring, for 1 more minute. Mix in 6 medium-size **tomatoes,** peeled and chopped; 1 teaspoon **sugar;** ½ teaspoon **salt;** and ¼ cup chopped **fresh basil leaves** or 1 tablespoon dry basil. Bring to a boil over high heat, stirring, and cook until tomatoes are soft. Reduce heat to medium and simmer, uncovered, stirring often, until sauce thickens and is reduced to about 3 cups (25 to 30 minutes).

Mushroom-Cheese Crêpes

France　　　　　　　　　　　　　　*Pictured on page 74*

Like the omelet, the French crêpe lends itself to a world of fillings. One classic combination is mushrooms with cheese, enlivened here with garlic, tarragon, and a splash of sherry.

　　Béchamel Sauce (recipe follows)
3　tablespoons butter or margarine
1　pound mushrooms, thinly sliced
1　shallot or green onion (including top), finely chopped
1　small clove garlic, minced or pressed
¼　teaspoon dry tarragon
1　tablespoon dry sherry
12　Whole Wheat Crêpes or Cornmeal Soy Crêpes (page 72)
½　cup whipping cream
1½　cups (6 oz.) shredded Gruyère or Swiss cheese
　　Freshly grated nutmeg
　　Tomato wedges (optional)

Prepare Béchamel Sauce.

Melt butter in a wide frying pan over medium-high heat; add mushrooms, shallot, and garlic and cook, stirring often, until mushrooms are lightly browned and liquid evaporates (8 to 10 minutes). Lift out about ¼ cup of the mushrooms; set aside for garnish. Sprinkle tarragon over mixture. Remove from heat and stir in sherry and half of the Béchamel Sauce. Spoon an equal amount of filling down center of each crêpe; roll to enclose. Place a single layer of filled crêpes, seam side down, in a lightly greased 9 by 13-inch baking dish. (At this point, you may let cool, cover, and refrigerate filled crêpes and sauce until next day.)

Add cream to remaining Béchamel Sauce and cook, stirring often, over medium heat until sauce is heated through. Pour evenly over crêpes, sprinkle with cheese, and dust lightly with nutmeg. Bake, uncovered, in a 425° oven for 12 to 18

(Continued on page 75)

Pancake, Crêpe & Tortilla Entrées　73

... Mushroom-Cheese Crêpes (cont'd.)

minutes or until lightly browned and bubbly. Spoon reserved mushrooms onto baked crêpes. Garnish with tomato wedges, if desired. Makes 4 servings.

Béchamel Sauce. Melt 4 tablespoons **butter** or margarine in a 1½ to 2-quart pan over medium heat. Stir in ¼ cup **unbleached all-purpose flour,** ¼ teaspoon **salt,** and a dash of **ground red pepper** (cayenne). Cook, stirring, until bubbly. Remove from heat and slowly pour in 2 cups **milk,** stirring until blended. Cook, stirring, until sauce bubbles and thickens. In a medium-size bowl, beat 3 **egg yolks.** Slowly pour in some of the hot sauce, stirring; then add egg mixture to sauce and cook over medium heat, stirring, just until sauce thickens but does not boil (about 1 minute).

Four-Cheese Crêpes

Italy

In their native Italy, these rich cheese crêpes are known as *crespelle quattro formaggi.* On your table, they're the foundation for an elegant supper.

- 1 cup (8 oz.) ricotta cheese
- 2 eggs
- ⅛ teaspoon *each* ground nutmeg and white pepper
- 4 hard-cooked eggs, pressed through a sieve or shredded
- ¾ cup grated Parmesan cheese
- 2 cups (8 oz.) shredded fontina cheese
- 1½ cups (6 oz.) shredded provolone cheese
- ¼ cup chopped parsley
- 16 to 18 Whole Wheat Crêpes (page 72)
- 4 tablespoons butter or margarine
  Chopped parsley

Beat ricotta cheese; stir in the 2 eggs, nutmeg, and pepper. Mix in hard-cooked eggs, ¼ cup of the Parmesan cheese, fontina and provolone cheeses, and the ¼ cup parsley. Spoon an equal amount of filling down center of each crêpe; roll to enclose.

Melt butter in a 9 by 13-inch baking dish in a 350° oven. Place a single layer of filled crêpes, seam side down, in melted butter. Bake for 15 minutes; sprinkle remaining ½ cup Parmesan cheese over top and

bake for 10 to 15 more minutes or until cheese is melted and browned. Garnish with chopped parsley. Makes 4 to 6 servings.

Summer Vegetable Enchiladas

Mexico

What the filled crêpe is to France, the enchilada is to Mexico: a plump and tasty pancake packet whose filling depends on the ingredients at hand—and the whim of the cook. These enchiladas are stuffed with a well-seasoned, brightly colored mélange of zucchini, corn, and bell pepper.

- 2 tablespoons butter or margarine
- 1 large onion, finely chopped
- 1 clove garlic, minced or pressed
- 2 large tomatoes, peeled, seeded, and chopped
- ½ teaspoon salt
- ¼ teaspoon *each* ground cumin and ground coriander
- 2 canned green chiles, chopped
- ½ cup tomato juice
- 1 cup whipping cream
- 12 six-inch Corn Tortillas (page 77 or purchased)
  Zucchini Filling (recipe follows)
- 1 cup (4 oz.) *each* shredded jack and medium-sharp Cheddar cheeses
- ½ cup Mexican Cream (page 54) or sour cream
- ¼ cup slivered ripe olives
- 2 green onions (including tops), thinly sliced

Melt butter in a wide frying pan over medium heat. Add onion and cook, stirring, until soft but not browned. Mix in garlic, tomatoes, salt, cumin, coriander, chiles, and tomato juice. Bring to a boil over high heat; cover, reduce heat, and simmer for 15 minutes. Uncover and return to a boil over medium-high heat, stirring often; continue boiling until sauce is reduced to about 1½ cups. Spread sauce in a 9 by 13-inch baking dish.

Heat whipping cream in a small frying pan over medium-low heat. Dip tortillas, one at a time, into hot cream to soften; remove from pan. Spoon an equal amount of Zucchini Filling down center of each tortilla; roll to enclose. Place a single layer of filled tortillas, seam side down, in sauce in baking dish. Pour any remaining cream over enchiladas. Sprinkle evenly with cheeses. Bake, uncovered, in a 375° oven for 20 to 25 minutes or until filling is heated through and cheese is melted and lightly browned.

Spoon Mexican Cream in a strip across middle of enchiladas. Sprinkle with olives and green onions. Serve immediately. Makes 4 servings.

(Continued on next page)

Bon appétit *is a foregone conclusion when your plate smiles up at you—especially if it's laden with Mushroom-Cheese Crêpes (recipe on this page) from France. Sauced with creamy Béchamel, our whole wheat wrappers enclose a sherried, garlicky filling. Marinated White Bean Salad (page 47), also French, complements the protein as well as the flavors.*

Zucchini Filling. Cut 4 small **zucchini** (about 1¼ lbs. *total*) into ½-inch cubes; you should have about 4 cups. Melt 3 tablespoons **butter** or margarine in a wide frying pan over high heat. Add zucchini; 1 cup whole kernel **corn**, cut off cob (about 2 small ears), or frozen and thawed; 1 red or green **bell pepper**, seeded and chopped; 1 medium-size **onion**, finely chopped; and 2 cloves **garlic**, minced or pressed. Cook, stirring often, until liquid evaporates and vegetables are tender-crisp (about 5 minutes). Season to taste with **salt** and **pepper**.

Zesty Black Bean Tacos

Guatemala

Hearty black beans are a popular ingredient in Latin American cooking, and when simmered with onion, garlic, and bit of red chile, they form the basis for a distinctive taco.

    Simmered Black Beans (recipe follows)
- 1 **head romaine lettuce (about 1 lb.), cut into shreds**
- 1 **large tomato, seeded and chopped**
- ½ **cup alfalfa sprouts**
- 1 **small red or green bell pepper, seeded and cut into strips**
- 1 **small can (2¼ oz.) sliced ripe olives, drained**
- 3 **green onions (including tops), thinly sliced, or ½ cup mild red onion, thinly sliced**

    Chili-Cumin Dressing (recipe follows)
    Salad oil
- 18 **six-inch Corn Tortillas (page 77 or purchased)**
- 2 **cups (8 oz.) shredded sharp Cheddar or jack cheese**

    Mexican Cream (page 54) or sour cream
    Guacamole (page 55)

Prepare Simmered Black Beans.

Place lettuce in a large salad bowl and top with tomato, sprouts, bell pepper, olives, and onions. Set aside.

Prepare Chili-Cumin Dressing and set aside.

Pour oil into a deep pan to a depth of ½ inch and heat to 350° on a deep-frying thermometer. Fry one tortilla at a time just until soft (about 10 seconds), then fold in half and, holding it slightly open with tongs, continue frying, turning, until entire surface is crisp and lightly browned (about 1 minute). Drain on paper towels. If made ahead, wrap tortillas with plastic wrap and store at room temperature until next day. Reheat on a baking sheet in a 200° oven for 10 to 15 minutes.

To serve, lightly toss salad with dressing. Let guests assemble tacos by spooning about 2 heaping tablespoons beans into a warm shell, then adding cheese and about ½ cup salad, and topping with Mexican Cream and Guacamole. Makes 6 servings.

Chili-Cumin Dressing. Stir together 2 tablespoons **red wine vinegar;** 1 clove **garlic**, minced or pressed; 1 teaspoon **chili powder;** ½ teaspoon *each* ground **cumin** and **salt;** and ¼ teaspoon **pepper.** Beat in ⅓ cup **salad oil** slowly until well blended. Makes about ½ cup.

Simmered Black Beans. Rinse and sort 1 cup **dried black beans.** Soak beans as directed on page 49.

Drain beans. Heat 1 tablespoon **olive oil** or salad oil in a 2-quart pan over medium heat. Add 1 medium-size **onion**, finely chopped, and cook, stirring occasionally, until soft. Mix in 1 clove **garlic**, minced or pressed; beans; 1 small **dried whole hot, red chile**, crushed; ½ teaspoon **salt;** and 2½ cups **water.** Bring to a boil over high heat. Cover, reduce heat, and simmer until liquid is absorbed and beans are very tender (2 to 2½ hours).

If made ahead, let cool, cover, and refrigerate until next day. To reheat, place pan over medium heat and cook, stirring often, until heated through (about 15 minutes). Makes about 3 cups.

Tomato-Avocado Quesadillas

Argentina

The Argentines have taken the unassuming—but tasty—tortilla and stuffed it with a colorful filling of zucchini, onion, chile, and cheese.

- 2 **tablespoons salad oil**
- 1 **medium-size onion, finely chopped**
- 2 **teaspoons minced fresh serrano chiles or jalapeño chiles**
- 1 **cup finely chopped zucchini**
- 8 **nine-inch Whole Wheat Tortillas or Flour Tortillas with Sesame Seeds (page 77), or purchased flour tortillas**
- 2½ **to 3 cups (10 to 12 oz.) shredded jack or mild Cheddar cheese**
- 2 **medium-size tomatoes, thinly sliced**
- 1½ **cups Guacamole (page 55)**

Heat oil in a wide frying pan over medium heat. Add onion and chiles and cook, stirring, until onion is soft. Stir in zucchini and cook, stirring, until zucchini is bright green and tender-crisp (3 to 4 minutes). With a slotted spoon, transfer zucchini mixture to a bowl. If necessary, use a paper towel to blot excess oil—pan should have just enough to keep tortillas from sticking.

Place a tortilla in pan over medium heat to

soften. Turn over; place about ⅓ cup of the cheese and about 2 tablespoons of the vegetable mixture on half of the tortilla. Fold the other half over filling and cook until cheese is melted and bottom of tortilla is lightly browned. Turn carefully and cook until other side is lightly browned. Remove from pan and keep warm while assembling and cooking remaining quesadillas.

Just before serving, spread each tomato slice with guacamole. Carefully open quesadillas and insert 2 or 3 guacamole-topped tomato slices in each. Makes 8 servings.

Wraparound Breads from Mexico

Following are three tortilla variations, starting with the traditional corn tortilla (made from *masa harina*). Next come recipes for flour tortillas (common in northern Mexico), one with sesame seeds for extra protein, the other made with whole wheat flour.

Look for a tortilla press in Latin American grocery stores or gourmet cookware shops.

Corn Tortillas

2 cups masa harina (dehydrated masa flour)
1¼ to 1⅓ cups warm water

Mix masa flour with enough of the warm water to make dough hold together. With your hands, shape dough into a ball. Divide into 12 equal pieces, then roll each into a ball.

Place a square of wax paper or plastic wrap on bottom half of tortilla press; place a ball of dough on paper, slightly off center toward edge farthest from handle. Flatten ball slightly with your palm. Cover with a second square of wax paper. Lower top of press (being careful not to wrinkle paper) and push down firmly on lever until tortilla measures about 6 inches in diameter. Stack paper-covered tortillas; repeat until all are shaped.

For each tortilla, peel off top piece of wax paper carefully. Place tortilla, paper side up, on a griddle or heavy frying pan preheated over medium-high heat. As tortilla becomes warm, peel off paper.

Cook, turning frequently, until tortilla looks dry (it should still be soft) and is lightly flecked with brown specks (1½ to 2 minutes)—it will puff up briefly.

Serve tortillas immediately, or let cool and wrap airtight. Refrigerate for up to 2 days or freeze for longer storage. Makes twelve 6-inch tortillas.

Flour Tortillas with Sesame Seeds

2 cups unbleached all-purpose flour
2 tablespoons nonfat dry milk powder
¼ cup sesame seeds
½ teaspoon salt
2 tablespoons butter, margarine, or solid shortening
¾ cup lukewarm water

Combine flour, milk powder, sesame seeds, and salt. With a pastry blender or 2 knives, cut in butter until mixture resembles fine crumbs. Slowly pour in water, mixing lightly with a fork. On a floured board, knead dough until smooth and elastic (about 5 minutes). Shape into a ball, cover, and let stand for 10 minutes.

Divide and shape dough into 8 balls for 9-inch tortillas, 12 balls for 6-inch tortillas. Keep balls covered to prevent them from drying out. On a lightly floured board, roll out one ball at a time as thin as possible. As each tortilla is shaped, place on a griddle or heavy frying pan preheated over medium-high heat. Almost immediately, blisters should appear. Use a wide spatula to press gently but firmly all over top. Blisters will form over most of surface as you press. Turn and cook other side until blisters are golden brown.

Stack cooked tortillas in a tightly covered dish or wrap tightly in foil to keep them soft. Serve warm; or let cool, wrap airtight, and refrigerate.

To reheat, wrap with foil and heat in a 350° oven for 15 minutes. Makes eight 9-inch tortillas or twelve 6-inch tortillas.

Whole Wheat Tortillas. Prepare **Flour Tortillas with Sesame Seeds,** but substitute 2 cups **whole wheat flour** for unbleached all-purpose flour. Omit milk powder and sesame seeds. Increase **butter** to 4 tablespoons; reduce **water** to ½ cup.

Crisp Burritos with Beans

Mexico

A specialty in northern Mexico, *chimichangas*—fried burritos—make a hearty entrée.

- 3 tablespoons salad oil
- 1 large onion, finely chopped
- 3 cloves garlic, minced or pressed
- 1 medium-size fresh jalapeño chile, cored, seeded, and finely chopped
- 1 teaspoon ground cumin
- 3 cups cooked pinto or black beans (page 49) or 2 cans (15 oz. *each*) pinto beans
- 1 tablespoon red wine vinegar
  Salt
- 16 nine-inch Whole Wheat Tortillas or Flour Tortillas with Sesame Seeds (page 77), or purchased flour tortillas
  Salad oil or solid shortening
- 4 to 5 cups shredded romaine or iceberg lettuce
- 1 cup (4 oz.) *each* shredded mild Cheddar and jack cheeses
  Guacamole (page 55)
  Mexican Cream (page 54) or sour cream
  Radishes
  Ripe Olives

Heat the 3 tablespoons oil in a wide frying pan over medium heat. Add onion, garlic, chile, and cumin; cook, stirring, until onion is soft and lightly browned. Drain beans well, reserving liquid; add beans to onion mixture. As beans heat, mash them with a potato or bean masher, mixing all ingredients to make a fairly smooth paste. Add bean liquid as needed (mixture should not become too dry). Add vinegar and season to taste with salt.

Soften tortillas by sprinkling each with a few drops of water and turning over several times in a nonstick frying pan over low heat. Spoon a scant ¼ cup bean mixture into center of each tortilla, wrap envelope-fashion, and fasten with a wooden pick.

Pour oil into a wide, deep frying pan to a depth of ½ inch and heat to 350° on a deep-frying thermometer. Cook filled tortillas, 3 or 4 at a time, turning, until lightly browned and crisp on both sides. With a slotted spoon, remove burritos and drain on paper towels. Keep warm in a 250° oven while frying remaining filled tortillas.

If made ahead, let cool, wrap airtight, and refrigerate until next day. Freeze for longer storage. To reheat, cover lightly with foil and heat in a 350° oven for 12 to 15 minutes if refrigerated (25 minutes if frozen). Place hot burritos on a bed of shredded lettuce, sprinkle with cheeses, and top with Guacamole and Mexican Cream. Garnish with radishes and olives. Makes 8 servings.

Vegetable-Bean Tostadas

Mexico   *Pictured on facing page*

Guests will love these make-at-the-table *tostadas*, especially since they have a choice of condiments to pile on top. The only problem is deciding which combinations of flavors and textures would taste best—shredded lettuce, tomato, peanuts, sour cream, taco sauce, or all of the above.

- Spicy Vegetable Filling (recipe follows)
  Salad oil
- 10 to 12 six-inch Corn Tortillas or Flour Tortillas with Sesame Seeds (page 77 or purchased)
- 2 cups (8 oz.) shredded Cheddar or jack cheese
- 3 cups shredded romaine or iceberg lettuce
- 1 large tomato, chopped
- 1 cup roasted peanuts or shelled sunflower seeds
  Mexican Cream (page 54) or sour cream
  Bottled red or green taco sauce

Prepare Spicy Vegetable Filling and keep warm.

Pour oil into a wide frying pan to a depth of ½ inch and heat to 350° on a deep-frying thermometer. Fry one tortilla at a time for about 30 seconds on each side, then drain on paper towels.

Let guests assemble tostadas by spreading filling on tortillas, sprinkling with cheese, then topping with lettuce, tomato, peanuts, Mexican Cream, and taco sauce as desired. Makes 5 or 6 servings.

Spicy Vegetable Filling. Heat 2 tablespoons **salad oil** in a wide frying pan over medium-high heat. Add 1 large **onion,** chopped; 2 large **carrots,** thinly sliced; 1 clove **garlic,** minced or pressed; 2½ teaspoons **chili powder;** 1 teaspoon **salt;** and ¾ teaspoon *each* **ground cumin** and **oregano leaves.** Cook, stirring often, until onion is soft (about 10 minutes). Stir in 4 medium-size **zucchini** (about 1½ lbs. *total*), cut into ½-inch cubes; 1 large **green or red bell pepper,** seeded and chopped; 1 cup whole kernel **corn,** cut off cob (about 2 small ears), or frozen and thawed; and 1 can (about 15 oz.) **red kidney beans,** drained. Cook, stirring often, just until zucchini is tender-crisp (7 to 8 minutes). Transfer to a warm serving dish.

Bright colors and bold flavors
announce a banquet of typically varied Mexican put-togethers. To put together a Vegetable-Bean Tostada (foreground— recipe on this page), you pile filling on a Flour-Sesame Tortilla (recipe on page 77); choose condiments ranging from chopped tomatoes and peanuts to shredded Cheddar and hot taco sauce. For a cooling dessert, there's Orange Flan (recipe on page 90).

Breads

Traditional staff of life in many cultures

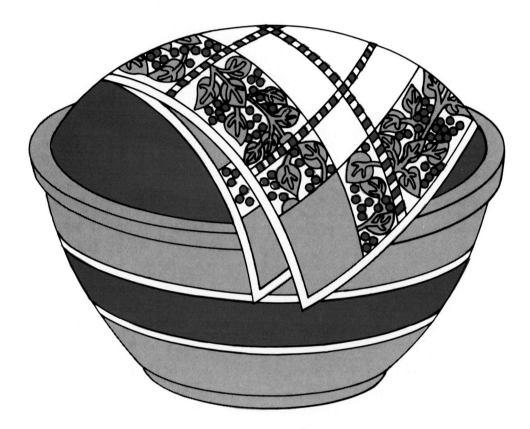

The incomparable aroma of fresh, hot bread wafting across the kitchen as you take it from the oven—such, surely, is one of the true comforts of home. It's a comfort to make and to bake, but the ultimate comfort is to eat it, with butter and honey or jam on top. And always it's a taste sensation that's vastly superior to its cellophane-wrapped counterpart sold from a shelf.

Our recipes are derived from traditional breads baked in brick, clay, and more modern ovens here and there across the globe. Occasionally, we've taken a liberty that most vegetarians will appreciate—substituting more heartily wholesome whole wheat flour for the white flour, but doing so always with an eye to retaining original ethnic flavor and character.

Where we have used all-purpose white flour, it is exclusively of the unbleached type. Not as heavily refined, unbleached flour creates a better-textured yeast bread. It's available in most grocery stores. Feel free, though, to substitute the bleached all-purpose flour that may be on your shelf, for the difference between the two flours won't be particularly noticeable in the finished product.

Yeast bread is made from a range of different flours, but whatever the flour, it must be one containing gluten, the component that is developed with kneading to give dough its elasticity. It is found in wheat flour and, in smaller amounts, in rye flour. Other flours, even rye flour, will not rise unless mixed with wheat flour.

If you're short on time, try some delectable quick breads. Our selection offers some interesting flavor variations—Country Corn Muffins from corn meal, for example—they're just briefly stirred, then baked immediately.

Country Corn Muffins

United States   *Pictured on page 38*

American Indians were the earliest bakers of cornbread; the Algonquin tribe called it "appone," from which Southerners coined the nickname "cornpone." Made from a wonderfully easy recipe—ideal for anyone new to bread baking—these southern muffins lend golden, grainy goodness to suppers and breakfasts alike. They complement such bean dishes as the Jamaican soup on page 37.

- 1 cup *each* stone-ground yellow cornmeal and unbleached all-purpose flour
- 2 teaspoons baking powder
- ½ teaspoon salt
- 2 tablespoons brown sugar
- 2 eggs, separated
- 3 tablespoons salad oil
- 1 cup buttermilk

In a medium-size bowl, stir together cornmeal, flour, baking powder, salt, and sugar. In another bowl, beat egg yolks, then stir in oil and buttermilk. In a third bowl, beat egg whites until soft, moist peaks form.

Add egg yolk mixture to cornmeal mixture, stirring only enough to moisten dry ingredients. Fold egg whites lightly into batter. Spoon batter into greased or paper-lined muffin pan with 2½-inch-diameter cups, filling each about two-thirds full. Bake in a 400° oven for 20 to 25 minutes or until golden brown. Turn out onto rack immediately. Serve warm. Makes 12 muffins.

Chapaties

India   *Pictured on page 19*

Stacked up alongside nearly every feast in India are these chewy, flat rounds of whole wheat bread. Their mild flavor helps cool the palate after the spicy fire of some Indian cooking. Made from the simplest ingredients, *chapaties* take about an hour to mix, knead, roll, and griddle-bake.

- 2 cups whole wheat flour
- 1 teaspoon salt
- About ⅔ cup warm water

In a bowl, stir together flour and salt. Stirring gently with a fork, add water slowly until a crumbly dough forms. With your hands, mix dough until it holds together. Add a few more drops of water, if needed. On a floured board, knead dough until smooth but still sticky (about 3 minutes). Wrap airtight in plastic wrap and let stand at room temperature for 30 minutes.

Divide and shape dough into 16 smooth balls and flatten each with your hand. On a floured board, roll each flattened ball into a circle about 5 inches in diameter. Stack circles, separating them with sheets of wax paper. If made ahead, seal in a plastic bag and refrigerate until next day.

Preheat an ungreased heavy frying pan or griddle over medium-low heat. Place a circle of dough in pan. After about 1 minute, top will darken slightly; at this point, press top of dough with a wide spatula. Blisters will gradually form and push up spatula; press them down. When bottom is lightly browned (about 1 more minute), turn bread over and cook until other side is lightly browned (about 2 more minutes). Place breads on a baking sheet, cover with a damp towel, and keep hot in a 225° oven while cooking remaining dough. Serve hot. Makes 16 chapaties.

Soda Bread

Ireland   *Pictured on page 82*

Crusty, yet cake-tender on the inside, soda bread appears routinely at Irish meals, from breakfast to high tea. The rounded slices make tasty partners for tea, soup, or eggs; lavish them with butter and honey or marmalade.

- 1 cup unbleached all-purpose flour
- 2 cups whole wheat flour
- 2 tablespoons brown sugar
- 1 teaspoon *each* salt and baking soda
- 2 tablespoons firm butter or margarine
- 1¼ cups buttermilk
- 1 tablespoon milk

In a large bowl, mix all-purpose flour, whole wheat flour, sugar, salt, and baking soda. With a pastry blender or 2 knives, cut in butter until mixture resembles coarse crumbs. Add buttermilk and stir only enough to moisten dry ingredients.

With floured hands, shape dough into a flattened ball about 2 inches high. Place on a greased baking sheet and brush top with the 1 tablespoon milk. With a sharp knife, cut an X in the top of the loaf to allow for expansion during baking. Bake in a 375° oven for about 40 minutes or until bread is golden brown and sounds hollow when tapped. Slide bread onto a rack and let cool slightly. Slice thickly and serve warm or at room temperature. Makes 1 loaf.

Raisin Scones

Scotland   *Pictured on facing page*

In the village of Scone, where Scottish kings were crowned in medieval times, these cakelike little breads were a royal favorite. Liberally laced with raisins and fragrant with spices, they're sure to be a favorite in your household, too.

    1 cup *each* unbleached all-purpose flour and
       whole wheat flour
    1 tablespoon baking powder
  1½ teaspoons ground cinnamon
    ½ teaspoon *each* salt and ground nutmeg
    ⅓ cup firmly packed brown sugar
    ⅓ cup firm butter or margarine
    ½ cup raisins or currants
    2 eggs, lightly beaten
    ⅓ cup milk

In a medium-size bowl, stir together unbleached flour, whole wheat flour, baking powder, cinnamon, salt, nutmeg, and all but 1 tablespoon of the sugar until well combined. With a pastry blender or 2 knives, cut in butter until mixture resembles coarse crumbs. Mix in raisins.

Measure 2 tablespoons beaten egg and set aside. Stir remaining egg and milk into flour mixture. Turn out on a floured board or pastry cloth and knead lightly just until mixture is smooth (about 6 turns). Pat into a circle about ¾ inch thick. Cut into 8 equal wedges and place wedges about 1 inch apart on a lightly greased baking sheet. Brush reserved egg over each wedge and sprinkle with remaining 1 tablespoon sugar. Bake in a 425° oven for 15 to 18 minutes or until well browned. Serve warm. Makes 8 scones.

Whole Wheat Baguettes

France   *Pictured on page 63*

Once or twice a day, the French buy up their 2-foot-long batons of bread, freshly baked in the ovens of local bakeries. Our whole wheat version isn't quite so long—but it easily fits both a standard pan and your oven at home.

A bit of Ireland and Scotland *come together for tea, with Soda Bread (center—recipe on page 81) from the Emerald Isle and Raisin Scones (recipe on this page) from the Highlands. In the traditional style, lavish both with sweet butter and jam.*

    1 package active dry yeast
    ¼ cup warm water (about 110°)
  1½ tablespoons sugar
    2 teaspoons salt
  1¾ cups warm water (about 110°)
    2 cups whole wheat flour
    4 to 4½ cups unbleached all-purpose flour
    ⅔ cup water
    1 teaspoon cornstarch

In a large bowl, dissolve yeast in the ¼ cup water and let stand until bubbly (5 to 15 minutes). Add sugar, salt, the 1¾ cups water, whole wheat flour, and 3½ cups of the all-purpose flour. Mix with a wooden spoon until flour is moistened and dough holds together. Turn dough out onto a board coated with ½ cup more of the all-purpose flour and knead until nonsticky, smooth, and satiny (10 to 15 minutes). Add more flour to board as needed to prevent sticking.

(Or use a heavy-duty electric mixer with a dough hook. Add whole wheat flour and 3½ cups of the all-purpose flour, then knead at high speed for 8 to 10 minutes, adding more all-purpose flour as needed to prevent sticking.)

Place dough in a greased bowl; turn over to grease top. Cover with plastic wrap and let rise in a warm place (80°) until almost doubled (1 to 1½ hours). Punch down dough, turn out onto a lightly floured board, and divide into 3 equal pieces.

Form each piece of dough into a smooth log by gently rolling dough back and forth until it is 10 to 12 inches long. Make a depression down center of each roll of dough; then fold dough in half lengthwise along depression. Seal along edge by gently pressing against fold with heel of your hand, rolling, and pushing sealed edge underneath.

With palms of your hands on center of loaf, begin rolling it back and forth rapidly, gently pulling from center to ends (as you slide your hands toward ends) until loaf is 15 to 16 inches long (length will depend on size of pan or baking sheet).

Place loaves in a greased triple baguette pan about 16 inches long, or place at least 1½ inches apart on a large greased baking sheet (12 by 15 inches or larger). Cover lightly with plastic wrap. Let rise in a warm place (80°) until puffy but not doubled (15 to 20 minutes).

Meanwhile, in a small pan, stir together the ⅔ cup water and cornstarch. Bring to a boil over high heat, stirring; remove from heat and let stand until slightly cooled. Uncover loaves and brush with cornstarch mixture, making sure to moisten sides of loaf down to pan or baking sheet.

With a flour-dusted razor blade, cut ½-inch-deep slashes diagonally across loaves at 2-inch intervals down length of loaves.

(Continued on next page)

Bake in a 375° oven for 15 minutes; then evenly brush loaves again with cornstarch mixture. Bake for 15 more minutes and again brush with cornstarch mixture. Bake for 10 more minutes or until loaves are golden brown and sound hollow when tapped (about 35 to 40 minutes *total*). Turn loaves out onto rack to cool.

For maximum flavor and freshness, serve bread the day it is baked. Or let cool completely, wrap airtight, and freeze; bread will regain its crispness when reheated. To reheat, place thawed loaves, uncovered, directly on rack in a 350° oven for 15 to 20 minutes. Makes 3 long loaves.

Sheepherder's Bread

Spain   *Pictured on page 58*

Tending flocks on windswept rangelands, miles from the nearest village, Basque sheepherders have had to develop virtuosity at campfire cookery. This large, dome-shaped loaf is but one example—cooked, like most of their food, in a cast-iron pot. Though Basques bury the pot under their campfire, ours goes less dramatically into an ordinary oven. If you want to be truly authentic, you'll have a loyal sheepdog nearby. Traditionally, the dog gets the first slice.

    3 cups very hot tap water (about 140°)
    ½ cup (¼ lb.) butter, margarine, or solid
       shortening
    ½ cup sugar
    2½ teaspoons salt
    2 packages active dry yeast
    8½ to 9 cups unbleached all-purpose flour
       Salad oil

In a large bowl, combine the hot water, butter, sugar, and salt. Stir until butter is melted; let stand until warm (about 110°). Stir in yeast, cover, and let stand in a warm place until bubbly (5 to 15 minutes).

Add 5 cups of flour and, with a wooden spoon or heavy-duty electric mixer at medium speed, beat until a thick batter forms. With a wooden spoon, stir in about 3½ cups more flour to make a stiff dough. Turn dough out onto a floured board and knead until nonsticky, smooth, and satiny (about 10 minutes), adding flour as needed to prevent sticking. Place dough in a greased bowl; turn over to grease top. Cover and let rise in a warm place (80°) until doubled (about 1½ hours).

Punch down dough, knead on a floured board until smooth, then shape into a ball. Cover the bottom of a 10-inch cast-iron or cast-aluminum Dutch oven (5-quart size) with a circle of foil. Oil inside of kettle, including foil, and underside of lid.

Place dough in kettle and cover with lid. Let rise in a warm place (80°) until dough pushes up lid about ½ inch (about 1 hour).

Bake, covered with lid, in a 375° oven for 12 minutes. Remove lid and bake for 30 to 35 more minutes or until loaf is golden brown and sounds hollow when tapped. Turn loaf out onto a rack to cool (you may need a helper). Peel off foil. Makes 1 large loaf.

Egg Bread

Israel   *Pictured on page 66*

The glossy, golden centerpiece of the Jewish sabbath, *challah* has been baked for so many centuries, and in so many places, that many variations exist. But every loaf is a light and fluffy braid, eggy and rich, and almost too good to believe.

    2 packages active dry yeast
    1½ cups warm water (about 110°)
    2 teaspoons salt
    2 tablespoons honey
    5 to 5½ cups unbleached all-purpose flour
    4 tablespoons butter or margarine, softened
    3 eggs
    1 egg yolk
    1 tablespoon water
    3 teaspoons poppy seeds

In a large bowl, dissolve yeast in the 1½ cups water and let stand until bubbly (5 to 15 minutes). Stir in salt and honey. Add 2½ cups of the flour and, with a wooden spoon or heavy-duty electric mixer at medium speed, beat until dough is elastic and pulls away from sides of bowl (about 5 minutes).

Beat in butter, then add eggs, one at a time, beating well after each addition. Stir in about 2½ cups more flour, about 1 cup at a time, to make a soft dough. Turn dough out onto a floured board and knead until smooth and elastic (10 to 15 minutes). Place dough in a greased bowl; turn over to grease top. Cover and let rise in a warm place (80°) until doubled (50 to 60 minutes).

Punch down dough and divide in half. Divide each half into three equal pieces and roll each piece into a rope about 14 inches long. Pinch tops of each group of three ropes together, braid to make a loaf, then pinch ends together. Place braided loaves several inches apart on a large greased baking sheet. Cover lightly with plastic wrap and let rise in a warm place (80°) for about 30 minutes.

In a small bowl, beat egg yolk with the 1 tablespoon water. Brush mixture lightly over each loaf, then sprinkle each with 1½ teaspoons of the poppy seeds. Bake in a 375° oven for 30 to 35 minutes or until loaves are well browned and sound hollow when tapped. Slide loaves onto a rack and let cool. Makes 2 loaves.

Garlic Cheese Bread

Italy   *Pictured on page 35*

Garlicky, cheesy, and with the consistency of pizza, *focaccia* is irresistible when served with hot soups and stews. It's pretty good on its own, too. Especially popular in Genoa, the flavorful bread is found throughout Italy, with regional variations.

    1   package active dry yeast
    1   cup warm water (about 110°)
    2   teaspoons sugar
    ¾   teaspoon salt
    ½   cup olive oil
    2⅔ to 3 cups unbleached all-purpose flour
    3   or 4 large cloves garlic, minced
    ¼   cup grated Parmesan cheese

In a large bowl, dissolve yeast in water and let stand until bubbly (5 to 15 minutes). Stir in sugar, salt, and ¼ cup of the oil. Add 2 cups of the flour, and, with a wooden spoon or heavy-duty electric mixer at medium speed, beat until batter is elastic and pulls away from sides of bowl (about 5 minutes). Stir in about ⅔ cups more flour to make a soft dough.

Turn dough out onto a floured board and knead until nonsticky, smooth, and satiny (10 to 15 minutes). Place in a greased bowl; turn over to grease top. Cover and let rise in a warm place (80°) until doubled (about 1 hour).

Heat remaining ¼ cup oil in a small pan over low heat; add garlic and cook, stirring occasionally, until soft and yellow (about 15 minutes). Set aside.

Punch down dough and knead briefly on a floured board just to release air bubbles. Roll dough with a rolling pin, then stretch it with your hands to fit bottom of a well-greased 10 by 15-inch rimmed baking sheet. Place dough in pan. With your fingers or tip of a spoon, pierce dough at 1-inch intervals. Drizzle garlic and oil mixture evenly over dough, then sprinkle with cheese. Let rise in a warm place (80°), uncovered, until dough is puffy (10 to 15 minutes).

Bake in a 400° oven for 15 to 18 minutes or until golden brown. Cut into 16 equal pieces and serve warm or at room temperature. Makes 16 pieces.

Rye Bread

Sweden   *Pictured on page 30*

In the chilly North, where rye grows better than wheat, *limpa* has long been Sweden's staff of life. A slice of this aromatic, plump loaf makes the ideal base for an array of Scandinavian open-faced sandwiches. Occasionally, caraway or fennel substitutes for the anise.

    2   packages active dry yeast
    ½   cup warm water (about 110°)
    2   cups milk
    ⅓   cup *each* molasses and firmly packed brown
         sugar
    2   tablespoons salad oil
    4½   to 5 cups unbleached all-purpose flour
    2   tablespoons anise seeds
    2   teaspoons salt
    2   cups dark or medium rye flour
    1   egg white
    1   teaspoon water

In a large bowl, dissolve yeast in the ½ cup water and let stand until bubbly (5 to 15 minutes). Meanwhile, in a small pan, combine milk, molasses, sugar, and oil; cook over medium heat, stirring, until sugar dissolves. Let mixture stand until warm (about 110°), then pour it into yeast mixture. Add 4 cups of the all-purpose flour, anise seeds, and salt. Stir until well blended, then beat with a wooden spoon or heavy-duty electric mixer at medium speed until smooth and elastic (about 5 minutes).

Mix in rye flour, about 1 cup at a time, and about ½ cup more all-purpose flour to make a soft dough. Turn out onto a floured board and knead until nonsticky, smooth, and satiny, adding all-purpose flour as needed to prevent sticking (8 to 10 minutes).

Place dough in a greased bowl; turn over to grease top. Cover and let rise in a warm place (80°) until doubled (about 1 hour). Punch down dough and shape into 2 round or long loaves. Place loaves 3 to 4 inches apart on a greased baking sheet (or shape dough to fit 2 greased 5 by 9-inch loaf pans). Cover lightly and let rise in a warm place (80°) until almost doubled (about 40 minutes).

In a small bowl, beat egg white with the 1 teaspoon water. Brush loaves lightly with egg white mixture. Bake in a 375° oven for 15 minutes, then reduce heat to 350° and continue baking for about 20 more minutes or until loaves are well browned and sound hollow when tapped. Let cool slightly in pans on a rack, then turn out onto rack to cool completely. Makes 2 loaves.

Whole Wheat Seed Bread

United States

Generously scattered through this whole wheat loaf, four kinds of seeds contribute both flavorsome crunch and extra nutrition. The bread has a coarse, but even, texture and is good plain or toasted. It requires only one rising and stays moist for several days if stored airtight at room temperature. Freeze for longer storage.

> 2 packages active dry yeast
> ¼ cup molasses or honey
> 1¾ cups warm water (about 110°)
> ¼ cup salad oil
> ½ teaspoon salt
> 4½ to 5 cups whole wheat flour
> ½ cup sunflower seeds
> ½ cup millet grains
> ¼ cup sesame seeds
> 2 tablespoons poppy seeds

In a large bowl, combine yeast, molasses, and water and let stand until bubbly (5 to 15 minutes). Add oil, salt, and 3 cups of the flour. With a wooden spoon or heavy-duty electric mixer at medium speed, beat until dough is elastic and pulls away from sides of bowl. Mix in sunflower seeds, millet, and sesame and poppy seeds. Turn dough out onto a board coated with 1½ cups more flour. Knead until flour is incorporated and dough is nonsticky, smooth, and satiny, adding more flour as needed to prevent sticking.

Shape dough into a smooth loaf and place in a greased 9 by 5-inch loaf pan. Cover lightly with plastic wrap. Let rise in a warm place (80°) until top of dough is about 1 inch above rim of pan (30 to 40 minutes).

Bake in a 350° oven for about 40 minutes or until loaf is browned and sounds hollow when tapped. Let loaf cool in pan on a rack for 10 minutes, then turn out onto rack and let cool completely before slicing. Makes 1 loaf.

Lemon Sweet Bread

Portugal

Lovely, lemony, and large, this impressive loaf from the Portuguese easily serves a dozen brunch guests. The soft, eggy dough conforms smoothly to the curves of fancy baking pans. Use either a decorative mold, or a bundt or tube pan that holds 2½ to 3 quarts.

> 1 small russet potato, peeled and thickly sliced
> Water
> 1 tablespoon milk
> 1 tablespoon butter or margarine
> 1 package active dry yeast
> ⅓ cup sweetened condensed milk
> ⅔ cup sugar
> 4 tablespoons butter or margarine, melted and cooled
> 3 eggs
> ¼ teaspoon ground mace or ground nutmeg
> 1 tablespoon grated lemon peel
> 4½ to 5 cups unbleached all-purpose flour
> Powdered sugar (optional)

Place potato in small pan; add water to cover. Bring to a boil over high heat and boil, partially covered, until very soft (15 to 20 minutes). Drain potato, reserving ¾ cup of the hot cooking liquid; let liquid stand until warm (about 110°).

Meanwhile, in a small bowl, mash or beat potato until smooth, then measure ½ cup potato and to it add the 1 tablespoon *each* milk and butter; stir until well blended.

In a large bowl, dissolve yeast in reserved cooled potato water and let stand until bubbly (5 to 15 minutes). Mix in condensed milk, sugar, melted butter, eggs, mace, lemon peel, and potato mixture. Beat until well combined.

With a wooden spoon or heavy-duty electric mixer at medium speed, beat in 4½ cups of the flour, about 1 cup at a time, to make a soft dough. On a floured board, knead until nonsticky, smooth, and satiny (about 10 minutes). Place dough in a greased bowl; turn over to grease top. Cover and let rise in a warm place (80°) until almost doubled (1 to 1¼ hours).

Punch down dough, turn out onto a floured board, and knead 2 or 3 times to release air bubbles. Grease and lightly flour a 10-inch tube pan. Shape dough into a 16-inch-long log and coil it into prepared pan so ends meet; pinch ends together to seal. Cover lightly and let rise in a warm place (80°) until almost doubled (about 45 minutes).

Bake in a 325° oven for 45 to 50 minutes or until bread is well browned and begins to pull away from sides of pan. Let cool in pan on a rack for 10 minutes, then turn loaf out onto rack to cool completely. Sift powdered sugar lightly over bread, if desired. Serve warm or at room temperature. Makes 1 large loaf.

Farm-fresh fragrance fills the kitchens of Indiana, Missouri, and other midwestern states when summer crops signal the pie-baking season. Our nut-crunchy Peach & Sour Cream Pie (page 91) tastes good enough to win the regional blue ribbon.

Desserts

From Boston to Budapest, people love sweets

N o matter where dinner is served—in Budapest, Ankara, or South Bend, Indiana—people appreciate a sweet dessert afterward. Desserts may be as plain as fruit or a custard —or they may be much fancier and sweeter. Even the most conscientious adherents to a wholesome diet occasionally get a craving for a very rich dessert—and indulging that now-and-then urge is said to be good for the soul.

In this chapter, we present a sampler of sweets enjoyed around the world. Most are easily made and are much lower in "empty" (non-nutritional) calories than the sugary extravaganzas many of us grew up with. We've included a full repertoire of favorite dessert forms, from the lightest of puddings and ices to more substantial cakes and pastries.

Generally, for menu balance, a fruity or other light dessert makes the most pleasant ending to a substantial or spicy meal, such as Latin or Indian dishes. On the other hand, when supper is a simple bowl of soup, you may want to play up dessert a bit more.

Season affects the choice of dessert, too. In summertime, after a patio picnic, Papaya-Lime Ice Cream would make a refreshing choice; in chilly January, though, you might prefer to offer warm Poached Apples with Almonds and Yogurt from Turkey.

Whatever appeals from our array of desserts, don't overlook our special feature "Coffees & Teas" on page 93. Here you'll find scented teas to serve with exotic fare, or rich coffee to enjoy with all sorts of desserts—such as a slice of Peach & Sour Cream Pie from the United States, or Almond Crescents from Greece.

Oranges in Orange Flower Water

Morocco

In Casablanca, this citrus celebration might arrive as a first-course salad—or, just as likely, as dessert. The dollop of orange-flavored yogurt on top makes it especially glorious. You can buy orange flower water at gourmet groceries or liquor stores.

    4 large navel oranges
    1 teaspoon orange flower water
       Ground cinnamon
    4 teaspoons powdered sugar
    ½ pint (1 cup) orange-flavored yogurt

Peel oranges with a knife, removing white membrane completely; cut between membranes and lift out orange in segments. Arrange each cut-up orange on a dessert plate so that segments resemble petals of a flower. Sprinkle each serving with ¼ teaspoon of the orange flower water, then cover with plastic wrap and refrigerate for at least 2 hours or until next day.

To serve, uncover, sprinkle each serving with cinnamon and 1 teaspoon of the sugar, and spoon ¼ cup of the yogurt into center. Makes 4 servings.

Fresh Berry Soup

Scandinavia

Summer or winter, Scandinavians perk up their spirits with rich fruit soups. This berry rendition is equally tasty for dessert or breakfast, hot or cold (it thickens to pudding consistency as it cools). Use any tart berry, such as boysenberries, raspberries, olallieberries, or currants. You can substitute frozen berries packed in sugar syrup, but if you do, don't use the sugar called for in the recipe. For a smoother, seedless soup, force the berry-sugar mixture through a strainer before adding the cornstarch.

    1   cup water
    ⅔   cup sugar
    4   cups fresh berries (see suggestions above)
    1½   tablespoons cornstarch
    2   tablespoons water
         Whipping cream or Mexican Cream
         (page 54), optional

In a 2 to 3-quart pan, combine the 1 cup water and sugar. Bring to a boil over high heat. Add berries and bring to a boil again. Cook for 1 to 2 minutes,

taking care that berries do not overcook and fall apart. Blend cornstarch with the 2 tablespoons water and stir into berry mixture. Stirring gently, return to a boil over high heat. Serve hot; or cool, cover, refrigerate, and serve cold. If desired, offer a pitcher of cream, or dollops of whipped cream or Mexican Cream. Makes 4 to 6 servings (about 1½ quarts).

Poached Apples with Almonds & Yogurt

Turkey

Typical of Turkey is this dessert in which cloves, almonds, yogurt, and a sugar syrup sing a quartet in praise of hot, cooked apples. A refreshing finale to a cool-weather meal, this dish is Ankara's answer to our own baked apples.

    ⅓   cup sliced almonds
    24 whole cloves
    6   medium-size tart green apples, peeled and
        cored
    ⅔   cup sugar
    1   cup water
    ½   cup plain yogurt
        Dash of almond extract

Spread almonds in a shallow pan and toast in a 350° oven for about 8 minutes or until lightly browned. Set aside.

Insert 4 cloves around top of each apple; set apples aside. In a wide 3 to 4-quart pan, combine sugar and water. Bring to a boil over high heat and cook, stirring, until sugar dissolves. Set apples in syrup. Cover, reduce heat to low, and cook, basting apples with syrup several times, until tender (12 to 15 minutes).

To serve, place each apple in a shallow dessert dish. Stir together yogurt and almond extract, and spoon into center of each apple. Spoon syrup around apples and sprinkle with almonds. Serve warm or at room temperature. Makes 6 servings.

Bananas Managua

Nicaragua

From the plantations that provide most of Nicaragua's wherewithal, here's a tropical delicacy that's quick and easy to prepare, but makes an elegant presentation.

(Continued on next page)

> 3 large, firm ripe bananas
> ⅓ cup orange juice
> 6 tablespoons firmly packed brown sugar
> 1 teaspoon ground cinnamon
> 3 tablespoons butter or margarine
> 2 tablespoons lime or lemon juice
> ¾ cup Mexican Cream (page 54) or sour cream

Peel bananas and slice diagonally ¼ inch thick. Pour orange juice into a small, shallow bowl. Mix brown sugar and cinnamon in another bowl.

Melt 1 tablespoon of the butter in a 9-inch frying pan over medium heat. Dip a third of the banana slices into orange juice and then into brown sugar mixture. Add to pan and cook until lightly browned and glazed on both sides (about 1 minute *total*). Spoon into 2 shallow dessert dishes. Repeat with remaining bananas. When all are cooked, add lime juice and any remaining orange juice and brown sugar mixture to pan. Cook over medium heat, stirring, until mixture boils and becomes syrupy (this happens quickly). Pour evenly over bananas. Top each serving with a dollop of Mexican Cream. Serve immediately. Makes 6 servings.

Ginger Yogurt

India

This classic of Indian cuisine—barely sweetened and ginger-tangy—is especially delicious after a feast of your favorite vegetarian curry. Serve it on its own or as a sauce for papaya, strawberries, seedless grapes, or kiwi fruit.

> 1½ cups plain yogurt
> ⅓ cup ginger marmalade or chopped crystallized ginger
> ⅓ cup firmly packed brown sugar
> 2 teaspoons lemon juice

In a bowl, combine yogurt, marmalade, brown sugar, and lemon juice; mix thoroughly. Cover and refrigerate for several hours to blend flavors. To serve, spoon into 4 small dessert dishes. Makes 4 servings (about 2 cups).

Molded Sweet Cheese

France

In France, cheese is an everyday dessert. A fancier-than-usual presentation, this creamy version is lightly sweetened. Its name is *coeur à la crème*, which means "heart of cream," and it looks and tastes marvelous, especially when served with fresh sweet cherries. Use a traditional heart-shaped ceramic mold (with drainage holes) or a natural-finish basket to give this dessert its classic form.

> ½ pint (1 cup) small curd cottage cheese
> 1 large package (8 oz.) cream cheese, softened
> ¼ cup powdered sugar
> 1 teaspoon grated lemon peel
> 3 tablespoons kirsch
> Sweet cherries or berries

Press cottage cheese through a fine wire strainer placed over a bowl. Add cream cheese to bowl and beat with an electric mixer or spoon until well blended. Mix in sugar, lemon peel, and kirsch.

Place several layers of cheesecloth (dampened and wrung out) in a 2-cup heart-shaped mold, allowing cloth to extend well beyond edges. Place mold in a shallow pan. Spoon cheese mixture into prepared mold and loosely fold cloth ends over mixture. Cover with plastic wrap and refrigerate for several hours or until firm. If made ahead, refrigerate until the next day.

To unmold, open cheesecloth and invert mold onto a serving platter. Remove mold and cloth. Surround cheese with cherries. Makes 6 servings.

Orange Flan

Mexico   *Pictured on page 79*

Like many Mexican favorites, flan is an idea imported from the Iberian Peninsula. But only in tropical areas of Mexico are you likely to discover this citrus version, *flan de naranja*.

> 1 cup *each* sugar and orange juice
> 2 tablespoons lemon juice
> 1 tablespoon grated orange peel
> 6 eggs
> Orange slices

Preheat oven to 350°. Make a hot water bath for flan by setting a 9-inch pie pan (1¼ inches deep) in a slightly larger pan. While holding pie pan down so it won't float, fill outer pan with just enough hot water to come up around pie pan. Then remove pie pan and put outer pan with water in preheated oven.

Place ¾ cup of the sugar in a small heavy pan over medium heat. As sugar begins to melt, tip and swirl pan until sugar is completely melted and syrup is a clear, medium-amber color. Pour syrup into pie pan and, using hot pads to protect hands, tilt pan quickly to let syrup coat bottom and sides. Set on a wire rack; caramel will harden rapidly.

In a large bowl or blender, combine remaining ¼ cup sugar, orange juice, lemon juice, orange peel, and eggs; beat or whirl until well blended. Set caramel-lined pan in hot water bath in oven; pour in egg mixture. Bake, uncovered, for about 25 minutes or until the back of a spoon pushed gently into center forms a crevice about ⅜ inch deep.

Remove pie pan from hot water and let cool slightly; then cover and refrigerate until cold. As flan cools, caramel liquefies. To unmold, loosen custard edge with a knife, then cover with a rimmed serving plate. Holding plate in place, quickly invert, turning out custard with caramel on top. To serve, cut into wedges; spoon caramel on top. Garnish with orange slices. Makes 4 to 6 servings.

Note: Flan may also be baked in a 1-quart charlotte mold. Coat bottom and sides with caramel as directed above. Hot water bath should be about 1½ inches deep when mold is in it. Bake flan in a 350° oven for 50 to 55 minutes.

Glazed Rice Tart

Belgium

Leave it to the Belgians to come up with a handsome *tarte de riz*. Glistening apricot jam laced with kirsch glazes its delicate custard, and a ring of whipped cream and almonds dresses up the edge.

> Whole blanched almonds
> 1 cup long-grain rice
> 1 quart (4 cups) milk
> About 6 tablespoons sugar
> ¼ teaspoon salt
> 2 eggs, separated
> 1½ teaspoons vanilla
> ½ cup finely chopped blanched almonds
> ¾ cup apricot jam, pressed through a sieve
> 2 tablespoons kirsch or 1 teaspoon vanilla
> Whipping cream

Spread whole almonds in a shallow pan and toast in a 350° oven for about 8 minutes or until lightly browned. Set aside.

Place rice in a bowl, add water to cover, and let stand for 1 hour. Drain well. In a 2 to 3-quart pan, combine rice, milk, 3 tablespoons of the sugar, and salt; bring to a boil, stirring, over medium heat. Cover, reduce heat to very low, and cook until rice is tender to bite (about 15 minutes); remove from

heat. Beat egg yolks with some of the rice mixture and return all to pan. Stir in the 1½ teaspoons vanilla and set aside.

In a bowl, beat egg whites until soft, moist peaks form. Gradually beat in 3 more tablespoons of the sugar and continue beating until mixture is stiff and glossy. Fold egg white mixture and chopped almonds into rice. Pour into a greased and lightly floured 10 or 11-inch quiche dish or other shallow baking dish of 6 to 8-cup capacity; spread evenly.

Bake in a 350° oven for 20 to 25 minutes or until custard is set and top is lightly browned. Meanwhile, in a small bowl, stir together jam and kirsch. Spread mixture over custard. Refrigerate for at least 4 hours or until next day.

To serve, whip cream, adding sugar to taste. With a pastry bag and star tip, pipe whipped cream around edge of tart (or spoon cream around edge in swirls to form a ring); arrange almonds in a ring atop apricot glaze. Cut into wedges. Makes 8 to 10 servings.

Peach & Sour Cream Pie

United States   *Pictured on page 87*

American fruit pies rank among the finest of the world's pastries. Though fillings change from pie to pie, crusts have remained fairly constant. Here, though, is an exception—a creamy peach pie with a nut-crunchy base.

> Nut Pastry (recipe follows)
> 2 eggs
> ½ cup sugar
> 1½ cups sour cream
> ½ teaspoon grated lemon peel
> ¼ teaspoon *each* salt, ground nutmeg, and ground ginger
> 4 medium-size peaches, peeled and sliced (about 5 cups)
> Crumbly Topping (recipe follows)

Prepare Nut Pastry. Roll out on a floured board and fit into a 9-inch pie plate. Trim and flute edge.

In a bowl, beat together eggs, sugar, and sour cream until smooth and well blended. Mix in lemon peel, salt, nutmeg, and ginger. Pour half the mixture into pastry-lined pie plate. Arrange peach slices on top, then cover with remaining mixture. Bake in a 400° oven for 20 minutes.

Meanwhile, prepare Crumbly Topping. Sprinkle evenly over pie and return to oven for 15 to 20 more minutes or until filling is set and crust is well browned. Let cool. Makes 6 servings.

(Continued on next page)

Nut Pastry. In a bowl, mix 1 cup **unbleached all-purpose flour**, ⅓ cup finely ground **nuts** (almonds, pecans, or walnuts), and ⅛ teaspoon **salt**. With a pastry blender or 2 knives, cut 2 tablespoons **solid shortening** and 4 tablespoons firm **butter** or margarine into flour mixture until it resembles coarse crumbs. Stirring gently, add 1½ to 2½ tablespoons cold **water**, a little at a time, until dough holds together. Shape dough into a ball.

Crumbly Topping. In a small bowl, stir together ¼ cup **unbleached all-purpose flour**, 3 tablespoons **brown sugar**, and ¼ teaspoon *each* **ground nutmeg** and **ground cinnamon**. With a pastry blender or 2 knives, cut 3 tablespoons firm **butter** or margarine into flour mixture until it resembles coarse crumbs.

Cheese Pastries

Hungary

Wherever in the world you get hungry, these delicate pastries are sure to satisfy so deliciously that you'll look forward to getting hungry again.

        Buttery Pastry (recipe follows)
1½ pounds (about 3 cups) farmers cheese or dry curd cottage cheese
 5 eggs, separated
1½ cups sugar
 ¼ teaspoon salt
 1 teaspoon vanilla
 ½ cup golden raisins
        Grated peel of 1 lemon
        Powdered sugar

Prepare Buttery Pastry and divide in half. Cover one portion and set aside. Press remaining portion evenly over bottom of a 9 by 13-inch baking pan.

In a bowl, combine cheese, egg yolks, ¾ cup of the sugar, salt, and vanilla. Beat until smooth. Stir in raisins and lemon peel. Set aside.

In another bowl, beat egg whites (including reserved egg white from pastry) until soft, moist peaks form. Gradually beat in remaining ¾ cup sugar and continue beating until mixture is stiff and glossy. Fold into cheese mixture and spread in pastry-lined pan.

On a lightly floured board, roll remaining pastry into a 9 by 13-inch rectangle and carefully place over cheese filling. With a fork, pierce pastry all over at 1-inch intervals.

Bake in a 350° oven for 1 hour or until pastry is lightly browned. Let cool on a rack. Sprinkle lightly with powdered sugar and cut into 2 by 2½-inch diamonds. Makes 24 pastries.

Buttery Pastry. Place 2 cups **unbleached all-purpose flour** in a bowl. With a pastry blender or 2 knives, cut 1 cup (½ lb.) firm **butter** or margarine into flour until mixture resembles coarse crumbs. Stir in 1 **egg yolk** (reserve white for filling). Stirring gently, add 2 to 4 tablespoons **milk,** a little at a time, until dough holds together.

Almond Crescents

Greece   Pictured on page 43

These buttery pastries, called *kourabiedes* in their native Greece, have counterparts in neighboring Turkey, and as far away as Austria and Mexico.

 ½ cup ground almonds
 1 cup (½ lb.) sweet butter or margarine, softened
 2 tablespoons powdered sugar
 1 egg yolk
 1 tablespoon brandy or ½ teaspoon vanilla
 2 cups unbleached all-purpose flour
 ½ teaspoon baking powder
1½ to 2 cups powdered sugar

Spread ground almonds in a shallow pan and toast in a 350° oven for 6 to 8 minutes or until lightly browned.

In a bowl, cream butter until light and fluffy. Add the 2 tablespoons powdered sugar and egg yolk, mixing well. Stir in brandy and almonds. In another bowl, combine flour and baking powder. Gradually add flour mixture to butter mixture, blending until smooth.

Pinch off walnut-size pieces of dough and shape into crescents. Place on ungreased baking sheets, spacing cookies about 1 inch apart. Bake in a 325° oven for 30 minutes or until very lightly browned. Place baking sheets on racks and let cookies cool for 5 minutes.

Sift about half the 1½ to 2 cups powdered sugar over wax paper and transfer cookies to it. Sift the remaining ¾ to 1 cup powdered sugar over top to cover cookies. Let stand until cool, then store in a tightly covered container. Makes about 30 cookies.

Filbert Chocolate Bars

Germany

In the town of Trier in Germany's Moselle Valley, these luscious nut-flavored morsels are known as *haselnussecken*.

1 cup whole unblanched filberts or almonds
    Press-in Pastry (recipe follows)
½ cup (¼ lb.) butter or margarine, softened
¾ cup sugar
1 teaspoon vanilla
3 eggs
2 tablespoons unbleached all-purpose flour
½ teaspoon ground cinnamon
¼ teaspoon ground nutmeg
2 ounces semisweet chocolate, grated

Spread nuts in a shallow baking pan. Roast in a 350° oven for 10 to 12 minutes or until golden beneath the skins; let cool. Whirl nuts, about a third at a time, in a blender (or whirl entire amount in a food processor) until finely ground. Set aside.

Prepare Press-in Pastry and press it evenly over bottom of a greased 8-inch square baking pan. Bake in a 350° oven for 12 minutes or until lightly browned.

Meanwhile, in a bowl, beat butter and sugar until well blended, then beat in vanilla and prepared filberts. Add eggs, one at a time, beating well after each addition. Stir in flour, cinnamon, and nutmeg until well combined.

Spread nut mixture evenly over baked pastry. Return to oven and bake for 30 to 35 more minutes or until browned and a wooden pick inserted in center comes out clean. Remove from oven and immediately sprinkle with chocolate. Let stand for about 30 minutes, then spread chocolate evenly over surface. When completely cool, cut into 1½ by 2-inch rectangles. Makes 24 bars.

Press-in Pastry. In a bowl, stir together ¾ cup **unbleached all-purpose flour** and ⅓ cup **powdered sugar.** With a pastry blender or 2 knives, cut 4 tablespoons firm **butter** or margarine into flour mixture until it resembles coarse crumbs. Stir in ¼ teaspoon **almond extract** and 1 **egg yolk** until blended.

Coffees & Teas from Around the World

Here—representing diverse cultures—are four classic methods of brewing your after-dinner coffee or tea to help bring dinner to a warm and satisfying close.

Turkish Coffee

Place 1½ cups cold **water** and 4 teaspoons **sugar** in an *ibrik* or small pan over medium heat. When water is hot and sugar has dissolved, add ¼ cup **pulverized coffee.** Bring to a boil over medium-high heat, let mixture froth, then remove from heat and let foam settle. Repeat the frothing process two more times. (For a milder version, allow coffee to froth up only once or twice.) Add a few drops cold **water,** without stirring, to settle the grounds. Spoon some of the foam into each of 4 demitasse cups, then pour in coffee. Makes 4 servings.

Latin Coffee

In a pan, combine 4 cups (1 qt.) **whole milk,** ¾ cup **ground coffee** (fine or regular grind), and 2 tablespoons **sugar.** Over medium heat, stir constantly until milk is scalding hot, but *do not boil.* Pour mixture through a coffee filter or damp cloth (wrung dry) to remove grounds. Add ½ teaspoon **vanilla.**

Whip ¼ cup **whipping cream** and sweeten lightly. Pass at the table. Makes 4 servings.

Japanese Green Tea

Fill an earthenware pot with hot tap water. Let stand until pot is heated through (about 5 minutes). Discard water.

Place 2 tablespoons **green tea** in pot. Pour in 4 cups **water** that is just below boiling point. (The Japanese say that tea water should not be boiling or the tea will taste flat.) Let steep for 2 to 4 minutes (depending on desired strength). Serve in Japanese teacups. Makes 8 to 10 servings.

Indian Spiced Tea

In a 3-quart pan, combine 6 cups cold **water;** 12 whole **cardamom pods,** and three 2½ to 3-inch **cinnamon sticks,** broken into pieces. Bring to a boil over high heat; cover and continue boiling for 10 minutes. Add 3 tablespoons **Ceylon tea;** return to a boil, then cover, reduce heat, and simmer for 2 to 3 minutes. Add ¾ cup **sugar** and 2 cups **milk;** stir until sugar dissolves; cover and simmer for 3 to 4 more minutes. Strain through a fine sieve; discard leaves and spices. Serve hot. Makes 6 servings.

Papaya-Lime Ice Cream

West Indies

In this recipe, papaya whips easily into an icy summertime dessert, worthy of being served in any paradise.

    2   cups (about 1 lb. *total*) chopped papaya
    ¼   cup fresh lime juice
    ½   pint (1 cup) whipping cream
    ½   pint (1 cup) half-and-half (light cream)
    1¼ cups sugar

In a blender or food processor, purée papaya. Add lime juice, cream, half-and-half, and sugar and whirl until blended. Pour purée into a bowl and cover with plastic wrap. Freeze until mixture hardens around edge (about 1½ hours).

With an electric mixer, beat mixture until smooth (or whirl in a food processor). Place plastic wrap directly on mixture and return to freezer until firm (several hours or until next day).

One hour before serving, beat or whirl again until soft. Return to freezer until firm. Makes 6 servings (4 cups).

Fresh Pear Ice

Canada

Canadian cooking abounds with fruit desserts, such as this lovely Victorian-style creation.

    1   cup sugar
    2   cups water
        Zest (colored part of peel) of half a small lemon, cut into strips
    1   inch cinnamon stick
    ½   teaspoon vanilla
    5   medium-size pears, peeled, cored, and chopped (about 5 cups)
    2   tablespoons lemon juice
        Fresh mint sprigs

In a 2-quart pan, combine sugar, water, lemon zest, cinnamon stick, and vanilla. Bring to a boil over high heat, stirring, and cook until sugar dissolves; continue boiling, uncovered, for 2 minutes. Add pears and bring to a boil again. Cover, reduce heat, and simmer until pears are very tender (about 15 minutes). Remove and discard lemon peel and cinnamon stick.

Transfer pear mixture to a blender or food processor. Add lemon juice and whirl until smooth. Pour into a 9-inch square pan and freeze until edges are frozen but center is still soft.

Spoon mixture into a large bowl and, with an electric mixer, beat until smooth and creamy (or whirl in a food processor). Transfer to a freezer container and place a piece of plastic wrap directly on sherbet. Cover container tightly. Freeze until firm (6 to 8 hours at 0°F or colder).

To serve, scoop into 6 dessert dishes and garnish with mint. Makes 6 servings (about 5 cups).

Caramel-Walnut Oatmeal Cake

Scotland

The Scots know that there's more to oats than oatmeal. One of many oaty creations in the teatime category is this caramel-and-walnut cake.

    1   cup regular or quick-cooking rolled oats
    1½ cups boiling water
    ½   cup (¼ lb.) butter or margarine, softened
    1   cup *each* granulated sugar and firmly packed brown sugar
    2   tablespoons molasses
    2   eggs
    1½ cups unbleached all-purpose flour
    1   teaspoon *each* baking soda and ground cinnamon
    ½   teaspoon salt
    ¼   teaspoon ground nutmeg
        Caramel Topping (recipe follows)

Place oats in a bowl and pour in boiling water; let cool to lukewarm. In another bowl, cream butter and gradually beat in granulated sugar and brown sugar. Mix in molasses, eggs, and oats.

In another bowl, stir together flour, baking soda, cinnamon, salt, and nutmeg. Add to oats mixture and beat until smooth. Spread evenly in a greased and lightly floured 9-inch square baking pan. Bake in a 350° oven for 50 minutes or until center springs back when lightly touched.

Meanwhile, prepare Caramel Topping. Remove cake from oven and immediately spread it with topping. Broil 4 inches below heat until topping is browned and bubbly (about 3 minutes). Let cool on a rack before cutting. Makes 12 servings.

Caramel Topping. In a 2 to 3-quart pan, combine 6 tablespoons **butter** or margarine, ¾ cup firmly packed **brown sugar,** and 3 tablespoons **half-and-half** (light cream); stir over medium heat until butter is melted. Add 1 cup *each* **flaked coconut** and chopped **walnuts.** Bring to a boil, stirring; continue boiling and stirring for 1 minute.

Index

METRIC CONVERSION TABLE

To change	To	Multiply by
ounces (oz.)	grams (g)	28
pounds (lbs.)	kilograms (kg)	0.45
teaspoons	milliliters (ml)	5
tablespoons	milliliters (ml)	15
fluid ounces (fl. oz.)	milliliters (ml)	30
cups	liters (l)	0.24
pints (pt.)	liters (l)	0.47
quarts (qt.)	liters (l)	0.95
gallons (gal.)	liters (l)	3.8
Fahrenheit temperature (°F)	Celsius temperature (°C)	5/9 after subtracting 32